The Wiersbe

BIBLE STUDY SERIES

D1114590

The

Wiersbe
BIBLE STUDY SERIES

LUKE 14–24

Take Heart

from Christ's

Example

David C Cook®

transforming lives together

THE WIERSBE BIBLE STUDY SERIES: LUKE 14—24
Published by David C Cook
4050 Lee Vance View
Colorado Springs, CO 80918 U.S.A.

David C Cook Distribution Canada
55 Woodslee Avenue, Paris, Ontario, Canada N3L 3E5

David C Cook U.K., Kingsway Communications
Eastbourne, East Sussex BN23 6NT, England

All Scripture quotations in this study are taken from the Holy Bible, New
International Version®, NIV®. Copyright © 1973, 2011 by Biblica, Inc.™ Used by
permission of Zondervan. All rights reserved worldwide. www.zondervan.com.

In the *Be Courageous* excerpts, unless otherwise noted, all Scripture quotations are taken from
the King James Version of the Bible. (Public Domain.) Scripture quotations marked NASB are
taken from the New American Standard Bible®, Copyright © 1960, 1995 by The Lockman
Foundation. Used by permission. (www.Lockman.org.); NKJV are taken from the New King
James Version®. Copyright © 1982 by Thomas Nelson, Inc. Used by permission. All rights
reserved; and WUEST are taken from *The New Testament: An Expanded Translation* by Kenneth
S. Wuest. © Copyright Wm. B. Eerdmans Publishing Co. 1961. All rights reserved.

All excerpts taken from *Be Courageous*, second edition, published by David C
Cook in 2010 © 1989 Warren W. Wiersbe, ISBN 978-1-4347-6499-7.

LCCN 2014937605
ISBN 978-0-7814-1037-3
eISBN 978-1-4347-0790-1

© 2014 Warren W. Wiersbe

The Team: Alex Field, Karen Lee-Thorp, Amy Konyndyk,
Nick Lee, Helen Macdonald, Karen Athen
Series Cover Design: John Hamilton Design
Cover Photo: iStockphoto

Printed in the United States of America
First Edition 2014

1 2 3 4 5 6 7 8 9 10

042714

Contents

Introduction to Luke 14—24 7

How to Use This Study 9

Lesson 1
The Dinner Guest (Luke 14) 13

Lesson 2
Joy and Riches (Luke 15—16) 29

Lesson 3
Things That Matter (Luke 17) 45

Lesson 4
A Few Lessons (Luke 18) 59

Lesson 5
Jerusalem (Luke 19—20) 75

Lesson 6
Tomorrow (Luke 21) 91

Lesson 7
The Arrest (Luke 22) 107

Lesson 8
Crucifixion and Triumph (Luke 23—24) 123

Bonus Lesson
Summary and Review 139

Introduction to Luke 14—24

Courage

In these chapters, we see our Lord steadfastly going up to Jerusalem to suffer and die. *Be Courageous* is not only a fitting title but also a fitting challenge to us in these difficult days in which we live.

Each of us has a "Jerusalem," a "Gethsemane," and a "Calvary" appointed just for us in the will of God. Like our Savior, we must set our faces "like flint" (Isa. 50:7) and do what God has called us to do. It may not be easy, but it will bring joy to us and glory to God.

To Jerusalem … and Beyond

The last thing our Lord did was to bless His people, and the first thing they did was to worship Him! The two always go together, for as we truly worship Him, He will share His blessings. He opened their lips not only to witness but also to worship and praise Him!

Dr. Luke opened his gospel with a scene in the temple (Luke 1:8ff.), and he closed his gospel the same way (Luke 24:53). But what a contrast between the unbelieving, silent priest and the trusting, joyful saints! Luke has explained how Jesus went to Jerusalem and accomplished the work of redemption. Luke's book begins and ends in Jerusalem. But his next book, the Acts of the Apostles, would explain how that gospel traveled from Jerusalem to Rome!

—*Warren W. Wiersbe*

How to Use This Study

This study is designed for both individual and small-group use. We've divided it into eight lessons—each references one or more chapters in Warren W. Wiersbe's commentary *Be Courageous* (second edition, David C Cook, 2010). While reading *Be Courageous* is not a prerequisite for going through this study, the additional insights and background Wiersbe offers can greatly enhance your study experience.

The **Getting Started** questions at the beginning of each lesson offer you an opportunity to record your first thoughts and reactions to the study text. This is an important step in the study process as those "first impressions" often include clues about what it is your heart is longing to discover.

The bulk of the study is found in the **Going Deeper** questions. These dive into the Bible text and, along with helpful excerpts from Wiersbe's commentary, help you examine not only the original context and meaning of the verses but also modern application.

Looking Inward narrows the focus down to your personal story. These intimate questions can be a bit uncomfortable at times, but don't shy away from honesty here. This is where you are asked to stand before the mirror of God's Word and look closely at what you see. It's the place to take a good look at yourself in light of the lesson and search for ways in which you can grow in faith.

Going Forward is the place where you can commit to paper those things you want or need to do in order to better live out the discoveries you made in the Looking Inward section. Don't skip or skim through this. Take the time to really consider what practical steps you might take to move closer to Christ. Then share your thoughts with a trusted friend who can act as an encourager and accountability partner.

Finally, there is a brief **Seeking Help** section to close the lesson. This is a reminder for you to invite God into your spiritual-growth process. If you choose to write out a prayer in this section, come back to it as you work through the lesson and continue to seek the Holy Spirit's guidance as you discover God's will for your life.

Tips for Small Groups

A small group is a dynamic thing. One week it might seem like a group of close-knit friends. The next it might seem more like a group of uncomfortable strangers. A small-group leader's role is to read these subtle changes and adjust the tone of the discussion accordingly.

Small groups need to be safe places for people to talk openly. It is through shared wrestling with difficult life issues that some of the greatest personal growth is discovered. But in order for the group to feel safe, participants need to know it's okay not to share sometimes. Always invite honest disclosure, but never force someone to speak if he or she isn't comfortable doing so. (A savvy leader will follow up later with a group member who isn't comfortable sharing in a group setting to see if a one-on-one discussion is more appropriate.)

Have volunteers take turns reading excerpts from Scripture or from the commentary. The more each person is involved even in the mundane tasks, the more they'll feel comfortable opening up in more meaningful ways.

The leader should watch the clock and keep the discussion moving. Sometimes there may be more Going Deeper questions than your group can cover in your available time. If you've had a fruitful discussion, it's okay to move on without finishing everything. And if you think the group is getting bogged down on a question or has taken off on a tangent, you can simply say, "Let's go on to question 5." Be sure to save at least ten to fifteen minutes for the Going Forward questions.

Finally, soak your group meetings in prayer—before you begin, during as needed, and always at the end of your time together.

The Dinner Guest
(LUKE 14)

Before you begin …
- *Pray for the Holy Spirit to reveal truth and wisdom as you go through this lesson.*
- *Read Luke 14. This lesson references chapter 1 in* Be Courageous. *It will be helpful for you to have your Bible and a copy of the commentary available as you work through this lesson.*

Getting Started

From the Commentary

Sabbath day hospitality was an important part of Jewish life, so it was not unusual for Jesus to be invited to a home for a meal after the weekly synagogue service. Sometimes the host invited Him sincerely because he wanted to learn more of God's truth. But many times Jesus was asked to dine only so His enemies could watch Him and find something to criticize and condemn. That was the case on the occasion described in Luke 14 when a leader of the Pharisees invited Jesus to dinner.

Jesus was fully aware of what was in men's hearts (John 2:24–25), so He was never caught off guard. In fact, instead of hosts or guests judging Jesus, it was Jesus who passed judgment on them when they least expected it.

—*Be Courageous*, page 17

1. Here we pick up Luke's story in the middle. We might know a lot about Jesus already, but for some of the people at this dinner, this might be their first encounter with Jesus. What impression would they get of Him here (Luke 14:1–14)? In what ways is Jesus a "dangerous" person to sit with at a meal or follow on the road?

2. Choose one verse or phrase from Luke 14 that stands out to you. This could be something you're intrigued by, something that makes you uncomfortable, something that puzzles you, something that resonates with you, or just something you want to examine further. Write that here.

Going Deeper

From the Commentary

Instead of bringing them to repentance, Jesus' severe denunciation of the Pharisees and scribes (Luke 11:39–52) only provoked them to retaliation, and they plotted against Him. The Pharisee who invited Jesus to his home for dinner also invited a man afflicted with dropsy. This is a painful disease in which, because of kidney trouble, a heart ailment, or liver disease, the tissues fill with water. How heartless of the Pharisees to "use" this man as a tool to accomplish their wicked plan, but if we do not love the Lord, neither will we love our neighbor. Their heartless treatment of the man was far worse than our Lord's "lawless" behavior on the Sabbath.

—*Be Courageous*, pages 17–18

3. Review Luke 14:1–6. Why did the Pharisees invite the afflicted man to such an important dinner? In what ways were they baiting Jesus? What are some of the ways we test God today?

More to Consider: Read the following Scripture passages: Luke 4:31–37; 4:38–39; 6:1–5; 6:6–10; 13:10–17; John 5:1–9; and John 9:1–41. How does Jesus violate the Sabbath traditions in each of these passages? Why would His enemies need any further evidence to attack Him?

From the Commentary

Jesus healed the man and let him go, knowing that the Pharisee's house was not the safest place for him. Instead of providing evidence against *Jesus*, the man provided evidence against the *Pharisees*, for he was "exhibit A" of the healing power of the Lord Jesus Christ.

The Lord knew too much about this legalistic crowd to let them escape. He knew that on the Sabbath day they would deliver their farm animals from danger, so why not permit Him to deliver a man who was made in the likeness of God? Seemingly, they were suggesting that animals were more important than people. (It is tragic that some people even today have more love for their pets than they do for their family members, their neighbors, or even for a lost world.)

Jesus exposed the false piety of the Pharisees and the scribes. They claimed to be defending God's Sabbath laws, when in reality they were denying God by the way they abused people and accused the Savior. There is a big difference between protecting God's truth and promoting man's traditions.

—*Be Courageous*, page 19

4. How did Jesus expose the false piety of the Pharisees and scribes? How does this show the difference between protecting God's truth and promoting man's traditions? What are some of the traditions we uphold today that could get in the way of our relationship with Jesus?

From Today's World

The modern church continues to struggle with legalism versus grace in a number of key areas, depending on the church tradition. This includes such potentially divisive topics as women in leadership and the appropriate relationship between politics and the pulpit. Every church deals with these things according to its interpretation of Scripture and has to consider what grace would look like in a given situation.

5. What are the controversial topics your church is dealing with? Why is there such diversity between churches when it comes to these issues? How does your church make decisions about rules? What role does grace play when a church is wrestling with one of these controversies? What's the difference between legalism and biblical truth?

From the Commentary

Experts in management tell us that most people wear an invisible sign that reads, "Please make me feel important"; if we heed that sign, we can succeed in human relations. On the other hand, if we say or do things that make others feel insignificant, we will fail. Then people will respond by becoming angry and resentful, because everybody wants to be noticed and made to feel important.

In Jesus' day, as today, there were "status symbols" that helped people enhance and protect their high standing in society. If you were invited to the "right homes" and if you were seated in the "right places," then people would know how important you really were. The emphasis was on reputation, not character. It was more important to sit in the right places than to live the right kind of life.

In New Testament times, the closer you sat to the host, the higher you stood on the social ladder and the more attention (and invitations) you would receive from others. Naturally, many people rushed to the "head table" when the doors were opened because they wanted to be important.

—*Be Courageous*, pages 19–20

6. How does the attitude described in the excerpt from *Be Courageous* betray a false view of success? How does social status remain a problem in our churches today? How are we to address concerns about social status in the church?

From the Commentary

Jesus does not prohibit us from entertaining family and friends, but He warns us against entertaining *only* family and friends exclusively and habitually. That kind of "fellowship" quickly degenerates into a "mutual admiration society" in which each one tries to outdo the others and no one dares to break the cycle. Sad to say, too much church social life fits this description.

Our motive for sharing must be the praise of God and not the applause of men, the eternal reward in heaven and not the temporary recognition on earth. A pastor friend of mine used to remind me, "You can't get your reward twice!" and he was right (see Matt. 6:1–18). On the day of judgment, many who today are first in the eyes of men will be last in God's eyes, and many who are last in the eyes of men will be first in the eyes of God (Luke 13:30).

—*Be Courageous*, page 21

7. What are the dangers of forming a "mutual admiration society"? How do our churches do that? How can we maintain a supportive community that is inclusive rather than exclusive?

From the Commentary

> In our Lord's time, it was not considered proper to ask poor people and handicapped people to public banquets. (The women were not invited either!) But Jesus commanded us to put these needy people at the top of our guest list *because they cannot pay us back*. If our hearts are right, God will see to it that we are properly rewarded, though getting a reward must not be the motive for our generosity. When we serve others from unselfish hearts, we are laying up treasures in heaven (Matt. 6:20) and becoming "rich toward God" (Luke 12:21).
>
> —*Be Courageous*, page 21

8. In what ways does our modern world's competitive nature potentially inhibit our ability to serve others? How does the "What will I get out of it?" attitude negatively affect our service to others? How can we maintain the unselfish attitude that Jesus had and share what we have with others?

More to Consider: In Jesus' day when you invited guests to a dinner, you told them the day but not the exact hour of the meal. A host had to know how many guests were coming so he could butcher the right amount of animals and prepare sufficient food. Just before the feast was to begin, the host sent his servants to each of the guests to tell them the banquet was ready and they should come (Esther 5:8; 6:14). In other words, each of the guests in this parable had already agreed to attend the banquet. The host expected them to be there.

How does this expectation play into the host's reaction to the guests' refusal to attend? What excuses did they give? How does this parallel the way we sometimes respond to invitations to participate in service or other church activities?

From the Commentary

Having prepared a great dinner for many guests, the host did not want all that food to go to waste, so he sent his servant out to gather a crowd and bring them to the banquet hall. What kind of men would be found in the streets and lanes of the city or in the highways and hedges? The outcasts, the loiterers, the homeless, the undesirables, *the kind of people that Jesus came to save* (Luke 15:1–2; 19:10). There might even be some Gentiles in the crowd!

These men may have had only one reason for refusing the kind invitation: They were unprepared to attend such a fine dinner. So, the servant constrained them to accept (see 2 Cor. 5:20). They had no excuses. The poor could not afford to buy oxen; the blind could not go to examine real estate; and the poor, maimed, lame, and blind were usually not given in marriage. This crowd would be hungry and lonely and only too happy to accept an invitation to a free banquet.

Not only did the host get other people to take the places assigned to the invited guests, but he also *shut the door so that the excuse-makers could not change their minds and come in* (see Luke 13:22–30). In fact, the host was angry.

—*Be Courageous*, pages 23–24

9. What message did Jesus' parable have for the proud Jewish people who were so certain they would "feast in the kingdom of God" (Luke 14:15)? What warning does Proverbs 1:24–33 give those who would treat God's call lightly? What motivates people today to treat such warnings lightly?

From the Commentary

Jesus seems to make a distinction between salvation and discipleship. Salvation is open to all who will come by faith, while discipleship is for believers willing to pay a price. Salvation means coming to the cross and trusting

Jesus Christ, while discipleship means carrying the cross and following Jesus Christ. Jesus wants as many sinners saved as possible ("that my house may be filled"), but He cautions us not to take discipleship lightly, and in the three parables He gave, He made it clear that there is a price to pay.

To begin with, we must love Christ supremely, even more than we love our own flesh and blood (Luke 14:26–27). The word *hate* does not suggest positive antagonism but rather "to love less" (see Gen. 29:30–31; Mal. 1:2–3; and Matt. 10:37). Our love for Christ must be so strong that all other love is like hatred in comparison. In fact, we must hate our own lives and be willing to bear the cross after Him.

—*Be Courageous*, page 26

10. What does it mean for you to be "carrying the cross"? How is this a way of identifying with Christ? What is the difference between simply calling yourself a believer and identifying yourself with Jesus daily?

Looking Inward

Take a moment to reflect on all that you've explored thus far in this study of Luke 14. Review your notes and answers and think about how each of these things matters in your life today.

> *Tips for Small Groups: To get the most out of this section, form pairs or trios and have group members take turns answering these questions. Be honest and as open as you can in this discussion, but most of all, be encouraging and supportive of others. Be sensitive to those who are going through particularly difficult times and don't press for people to speak if they're uncomfortable doing so.*

11. What are some traditions you uphold? Do any of them get in the way of your relationship with God or your love for others? Why are those traditions so important to you? How can you respect a tradition while ensuring that it doesn't keep you from loving God and others well?

12. What is your goal when you serve others? Do you ever find yourself wondering what you'll get out of it? If so, what prompts that way of thinking? How can you avoid selfish thinking when offering yourself to others?

13. What are some ways you are "carrying the cross" in your daily faith life? What challenges do you face as you consider what it means to carry the cross? What are some ways you can find the strength to carry the cross when doing so seems too costly?

Going Forward

14. Think of one or two things that you have learned that you'd like to work on in the coming week. Remember that this is all about quality, not quantity. It's better to work on one specific area of life and do it well than to work on many and do poorly (or to be so overwhelmed that you simply don't try).

Do you want to practice identifying with Christ in your daily life? Be specific. Go back through Luke 14 and put a star next to the phrase or verse that is most encouraging to you. Consider memorizing this verse.

Real-Life Application Ideas: This week, take a look at all the ways you're living out what it means to be a follower of Christ. Then consider what it would look like if you were more than just a follower, but instead a dedicated disciple. What changes would you have to make to be a disciple? How can you go about making those changes? Make a plan to focus on the disciplines that will bring you closer to Jesus, not just those that define you as a Christian.

Seeking Help

15. Write a prayer below (or simply pray one in silence), inviting God to work on your mind and heart in those areas you've noted in the Going Forward section. Be honest about your desires and fears.

Notes for Small Groups:

- *Look for ways to put into practice the things you wrote in the Going Forward section. Talk with other group members about your ideas and commit to being accountable to one another.*

- *During the coming week, ask the Holy Spirit to continue to reveal truth to you from what you've read and studied.*

- *Before you start the next lesson, read Luke 15—16. For more in-depth lesson preparation, read chapters 2 and 3, "The Joys of Salvation" and "The Right and Wrong of Riches," in* Be Courageous.

Joy and Riches
(LUKE 15—16)

Before you begin …

- *Pray for the Holy Spirit to reveal truth and wisdom as you go through this lesson.*
- *Read Luke 15—16. This lesson references chapters 2 and 3 in* Be Courageous. *It will be helpful for you to have your Bible and a copy of the commentary available as you work through this lesson.*

Getting Started

From the Commentary

The story about the lost sheep would touch the hearts of the men and boys in the crowd, and the women and girls would appreciate the story about the coin that was lost from the wedding necklace. Jesus sought to reach everybody's heart.

The sheep in 15:3–7 was lost because of foolishness. Sheep have a tendency to go astray, and that is why they need a shepherd (Isa. 53:6; 1 Peter 2:25). The scribes and Pharisees had no problem seeing the publicans and sinners as "lost sheep," but they would not apply that image to themselves! And yet the prophet made it clear that all of us have sinned and gone astray, and that includes religious people.

The shepherd was responsible for each sheep; if one was missing, the shepherd had to pay for it unless he could prove that it was killed by a predator (see Gen. 31:38–39; Ex. 22:10–13; Amos 3:12). This explains why he would leave the flock with the other shepherds, go and search for the missing animal, and then rejoice when he found it. Not to find the lost sheep meant money out of his own pocket, plus the disgrace of being known as a careless shepherd.

—*Be Courageous*, page 32

1. What message was the shepherd giving by leaving the ninety-nine (Luke 15:4)? What message was Jesus giving about the scribes and Pharisees in this parable? What is the message here for us today?

More to Consider: There is a fourfold joy expressed when a lost sinner comes to the Savior. Though nothing is said in the story about how the sheep felt, there is certainly joy in the heart of the person found. Both Scripture (Acts 3:8; 8:39) and our own personal experience verify the joy of salvation.

2. Choose one verse or phrase from Luke 15—16 that stands out to you. This could be something you're intrigued by, something that makes you uncomfortable, something that puzzles you, something that resonates with you, or just something you want to examine further. Write that here.

Going Deeper

From the Commentary

> We call this story "the parable of the prodigal son" (the word *prodigal* means "wasteful"), but it could also be called "the parable of the loving father," for it emphasizes the graciousness of the father more than the sinfulness of the son. Unlike the shepherd and the woman in the previous parables, the father did not go out to seek the son, but it was the memory of his father's goodness that brought the boy to repentance and forgiveness (see Rom. 2:4).
>
> —*Be Courageous*, pages 34–35

3. Review Luke 15:11–24. Note the three experiences of the younger son: (1) rebellion (vv. 11–16); (2) repentance (vv. 17–19); and (3) rejoicing (vv. 20–24). How does he experience each of these? What motivates the son's repentance? What do these three experiences reveal about the father? The father's relationship with his son?

From the Commentary

It is interesting to consider the father's description of his son's experience: He was dead, and was now alive; he was lost, and now was found. This is the spiritual experience of every lost sinner who comes to the Father through faith in Jesus Christ (John 5:24; Eph. 2:1–10). Note the parallels between the prodigal's coming to the father and our coming to the Father through Christ (John 14:6):

The Prodigal	*Jesus Christ*
He was lost (v. 24)	"I am the way"
He was ignorant (v. 17)	"I am the truth"
He was dead (v. 24)	"I am the life"

—*Be Courageous*, page 38

4. What do the parallels described reveal about Jesus' love for prodigals? What does this parable teach us about those who seem totally lost? What role does faith play in this story? In our own story as we deal with those who have wandered astray?

From the Commentary

At this point in the parable, the scribes and Pharisees felt confident that they had escaped our Lord's judgment, for He had centered His attention on the publicans and sinners, pictured by the prodigal son. But Jesus continued the story and introduced the elder brother, who is a clear illustration of the scribes and Pharisees. The publicans and sinners were guilty of the obvious sins of the flesh, but the Pharisees and scribes were guilty of sins of the spirit (2 Cor. 7:1). Their outward actions may have been blameless, but their inward attitudes were abominable (see Matt. 23:25–28).

We must admit that the elder brother had some virtues that are commendable. He worked hard and always obeyed his father. He never brought disgrace either to the home or to the village, and apparently he had enough

friends so that he could have planned an enjoyable party
(Luke 15:29). He seems like a good, solid citizen and,
compared to his younger brother, almost a saint.

—*Be Courageous*, page 39

5. Review Luke 15:25–32. How are obedience and diligence good tests of
character? What is an even better test of character? (See Luke 10:25–28.)
Why is character important? What are the unique characteristics of a godly
character?

From the Commentary

The *Wall Street Journal* quoted an anonymous wit who
defined *money* as "an article which may be used as a
universal passport to everywhere except heaven, and as a
universal provider for everything except happiness." The
writer might have added that money is also a provoker of
covetousness and competition, a wonderful servant but
a terrible master. The love of money is still "a root of all
kinds of evil" (1 Tim. 6:10 NKJV) and has helped fill our
world with corruption and lust (1 Peter 1:4).

When you read our Lord's sermons and parables, you are struck with the fact that He had a great deal to say about material wealth. He ministered to people who, for the most part, were poor and who thought that acquiring more wealth was the solution to all their problems. Jesus was not blind to the needs of the poor, and by His example and teaching, He encouraged His followers to share what they had with others. The early church was a fellowship of people who willingly shared their possessions with the less fortunate (Acts 2:44–47; 4:33–37).

In His portrait of the prodigal and the elder brother, Jesus described two opposite philosophies of life. Prior to his repentance, the prodigal *wasted* his life, but his elder brother only *spent* his life as a faithful drudge. Both attitudes are wrong, for the Christian approach to life is that we should *invest* our lives for the good of others and the glory of God. This chapter emphasizes that truth: Life is a stewardship, and we must use our God-given opportunities faithfully. One day we must give an account to the Lord of what we have done with all He has given to us, so we had better heed what Jesus says in this chapter about the right and wrong use of wealth.

—*Be Courageous*, pages 45–46

6. What opposite philosophies did Jesus describe in His portrait of the prodigal and his older brother? What was wrong about both approaches to life? How does this chapter convey the idea that "life is a stewardship"?

From the Commentary

A steward is someone who manages another's wealth. He does not own that wealth himself, but he has the privilege of enjoying it and using it for the profit of his master. The most important thing about a steward is that he serve his master faithfully (1 Cor. 4:2). When he looks at the riches around him, the steward must remember that they belong to his master, not to him personally, and that they must be used in a way that will please and profit the master.

The steward in 16:1–2 *forgot* that he was a steward and began to act as if he were the owner. He became a "prodigal steward" who wasted his master's wealth. His master heard about it and immediately asked for an inventory of his goods and an audit of his books. He also fired his steward.

Before we judge this man too severely, let's examine our own lives to see how faithful we have been as stewards of what God has given to us. To begin with, we are stewards of the *material wealth* that we have, whether much or little, and we will one day have to answer to God for the way we have acquired it and used it.

—*Be Courageous*, page 46

7. In what ways does Christian stewardship go beyond paying God a tithe of our income? (See 1 Pet. 4:10; 1 Thess. 2:4; Rom. 14:10–12.) What does a faithful steward look like in daily practice?

From the Commentary

> In 16:3–8, the steward knew he would lose his job. He
> could not change the past, but he could prepare for the
> future. How? By making friends of his master's creditors
> so that they would take him in when his master threw
> him out. He gave each of them a generous discount, pro-
> vided they paid up immediately, and they were only too
> glad to cooperate. Even his master complimented him on
> his clever plan (Luke 16:8).
>
> —*Be Courageous*, page 48

8. What did Jesus commend the steward for? In what ways are "the people
of this world" (Luke 16:8) experts at seizing opportunities for making
money and friends and getting ahead? How can Christians apply a similar
kind of diligence to the spiritual affairs of life? How should the fact that
believers are investing in eternity affect the way they approach matters of
faith and finance?

More to Consider: How is it significant that both Paul and Peter use the words "dishonest gain"? (See 1 Tim. 3:8; Titus 1:7, 11; 1 Pet. 5:2.) Why is our Lord so concerned about the way we use money? What happens when we let money, not God, control our lives? Where in history has this been true? What lessons did we learn from these events?

From the Commentary

Jesus had been speaking primarily to His disciples, but the Pharisees had been listening, and their response was anything but spiritual. They sneered at Him! (The Greek word means "to turn up one's nose.") In spite of their strict religious practices, they loved money and cultivated values that were godless. They professed to trust God, but they measured life by wealth and possessions, the same as the unbelieving worldly crowd. *Far too many professed Christians today are making the same mistake.* With their lips, they honor the Lord, but with their wealth, they live like the world.

The Pharisees needed to stop "drifting" with the crowd and start "pressing into the kingdom" as many others were doing. The Pharisees had rejected the ministry of John the Baptist and permitted him to be killed, even though they knew he was God's prophet. They were also rejecting the ministry of Jesus Christ and would ultimately ask Pilate to have Him crucified.

—*Be Courageous*, pages 50–51

9. What happens to someone when his or her life is controlled by money? How can such control lead to a life of sin? Is that inevitable? Why or why not? How can those with lots of wealth live according to Jesus' teachings?

From the Commentary

The King James Version uses the word *hell* in Luke 16:23, but the Greek word is not "hell" but "hades." It is the temporary realm of the dead as they await the judgment. The permanent place of punishment for the lost is "hell," the lake of fire. One day, death will give up the bodies and hades will give up the souls (Rev. 20:13, where "hell" should be "hades"), and the lost will stand before Christ in judgment (Rev. 20:10–15)....

People ask, "How can a loving God even permit such a place as hell to exist, let alone send people there?" But in asking that question, they reveal that they do not understand either the love of God or the wickedness of sin. God's love is a *holy* love ("God is light," 1 John 1:5), not a shallow sentiment, and sin is rebellion against a holy and loving God. God does not "send people to hell." They send themselves there by refusing to heed

His call and believe in His Son. The "unbelieving" are named second on the list of the people who go to hell, even before the murderers and the liars (Rev. 21:8; also see John 3:18–21, 36).

Abraham gave two reasons why Lazarus could not bring the comfort that was requested: the character of the rich man and the character of the eternal state. The rich man had lived for the "good things" of earth, and had experienced abundant temporal blessings. He had his reward (Matt. 6:2, 5, 16). He had determined his own destiny by leaving God out of his life, and now neither his character nor his destiny could be changed. Lazarus could not leave his place of comfort and make even a brief visit to the place of torment.

Then the rich man prayed for his brothers (Luke 16:27–31). He did not say, "I'm glad my brothers will also come here. We'll have a wonderful time together!" Occasionally you hear a lost person say, "Well, I don't mind if I go to hell. I'll have a lot of company!" *But there is no friendship or "company" in hell!* Hell is a place of torment and loneliness. It is not an eternal New Year's Eve party at which sinners have a good time doing what they used to do on earth.

—*Be Courageous*, pages 53–55

10. Read Luke 16:28. Why is Lazarus's testimony so important? What impact did it have on the rich man? What was the great chasm between the

rich man and heaven? What does this chasm look like today? Why don't people believe even if someone rises from the dead (16:31)?

Looking Inward

Take a moment to reflect on all that you've explored thus far in this study of Luke 15–16. Review your notes and answers and think about how each of these things matters in your life today.

> *Tips for Small Groups: To get the most out of this section, form pairs or trios and have group members take turns answering these questions. Be honest and as open as you can in this discussion, but most of all, be encouraging and supportive of others. Be sensitive to those who are going through particularly difficult times and don't press for people to speak if they're uncomfortable doing so.*

11. Have you ever left the ninety-nine to find one lost soul? Who was the one you went after, and why was it so important to do that? How does your love for each person play out in practical ways?

12. If you've ever been a prodigal, describe what led to that season of life. Why did you leave? What brought you back? How did others respond to your leaving? To your returning?

13. What struggles do you have with faithful giving? What kind of giving is hardest for you? Time? Talent? Money? Why is that a challenge for you?

Going Forward

14. Think of one or two things that you have learned that you'd like to work on in the coming week. Remember that this is all about quality, not quantity. It's better to work on one specific area of life and do it well than to work on many and do poorly (or to be so overwhelmed that you simply don't try).

Do you want to learn how to be a more faithful steward? Be specific. Go back through Luke 15—16 and put a star next to the phrase or verse that is most encouraging to you. Consider memorizing this verse.

Real-Life Application Ideas: This week, take a close look at your time, talent, and treasure budgets. Consider how you're spending all three in relationship to your spiritual life. Are there ways you can better spend each of them in order to grow your faith and live out the Great Commission? If so, consider making some changes to accomplish this. Even a small change can make a big difference in your life and the lives of those whom you encounter daily.

Seeking Help

15. Write a prayer below (or simply pray one in silence), inviting God to work on your mind and heart in those areas you've noted in the Going Forward section. Be honest about your desires and fears.

Notes for Small Groups:

- *Look for ways to put into practice the things you wrote in the Going Forward section. Talk with other group members about your ideas and commit to being accountable to one another.*

- *During the coming week, ask the Holy Spirit to continue to reveal truth to you from what you've read and studied.*

- *Before you start the next lesson, read Luke 17. For more in-depth lesson preparation, read chapter 4, "Things That Really Matter," in* Be Courageous.

Things That Matter
(LUKE 17)

Before you begin …
- *Pray for the Holy Spirit to reveal truth and wisdom as you go through this lesson.*
- *Read Luke 17. This lesson references chapter 4 in* Be Courageous. *It will be helpful for you to have your Bible and a copy of the commentary available as you work through this lesson.*

Getting Started

From the Commentary

As Jesus made His way to Jerusalem, He continued to teach His disciples and prepare them for what He would suffer there. But He was also preparing them for the time when He would no longer be with them and they would be ministering to others in His place. It was a critical period in their lives.

In this chapter, Luke recorded lessons that Jesus gave His disciples about some of the essentials of the Christian life: forgiveness (Luke 17:1–6), faithfulness (Luke 17:7–10), thankfulness (Luke 17:11–19), and preparedness (Luke 17:20–37).

—*Be Courageous*, page 59

1. How are forgiveness, faithfulness, thankfulness, and preparedness each essential to a disciple's daily life? How do they help grow a disciple's faith?

2. Choose one verse or phrase from Luke 17 that stands out to you. This could be something you're intrigued by, something that makes you uncomfortable, something that puzzles you, something that resonates with you, or just something you want to examine further. Write that here.

Going Deeper

From the Commentary

> After Jesus warned the Pharisees about the sin of loving
> money (Luke 16:14–31), He then turned to His disciples
> to warn them about possible sins in their lives, for occa-
> sions to stumble ("offenses") are an unfortunate part of
> life. After all, we are all sinners living in a sinful world.
> But we must take heed not to cause others to stumble,
> for it is a serious thing to sin against a fellow believer and
> tempt him or her to sin (Rom. 14:13; 1 Cor. 10:32; 1 John
> 2:10).
>
> —*Be Courageous*, page 59

3. Review Luke 17:1–6. Why does Jesus place so much importance on
forgiveness? What is the purpose of forgiveness? Why would the young
believers have struggled with forgiving others?

More to Consider: By "these little ones" (Luke 17:2), Jesus was not only referring to children but also to young believers who were learning how to follow the Lord (see Matt. 18:1–6; Luke 10:21). Why did Jesus speak this way about young believers? What might have caused them to stumble? Why is the sin of causing someone to stumble so significant?

From the Commentary

Suppose another believer sins against you. Jesus anticipated this question in Luke 17:3–4 and instructed us what to do. First, we must have a personal concern for each other and obey His warning, "Take heed to yourselves." This means that we should lovingly watch over each other and do all we can to keep one another from sinning.

—*Be Courageous*, page 60

4. What is the proper way to deal with a brother or sister who sins against us? Why is it so easy to nurse a grudge when someone wrongs us? Why is this the wrong approach? (See Matt. 18:15–20.) What is a good first step toward solving personal differences? (See Eph. 4:15.)

From Today's World

Today's world is dramatically different from when Jesus walked the earth. Back then rumor was rampant, but rumor spread at the speed of papyrus and courier. Today, any news can travel as fast as a keyboard click. Social media can be anything but social when someone feels wronged and spreads that sentiment to friends, family, and a host of strangers. Because people often react before they think, it's far too common to have to backtrack or apologize for words that were spoken out of anger or hurt. Once they're out there, it's hard to make them disappear.

5. Why do we tend to react irrationally when we're wronged or hurt? How does a bad reaction to being hurt actually cause more hurt rather than make us feel better? What are some good practices to put in place so we don't overreact and make a bad situation worse by sharing it inappropriately?

From the Commentary

The introductory word *but* in 17:7 indicates that Jesus was now going to balance one lesson with another. There was a danger that the Twelve might get so carried away with transplanting trees that they would ignore the everyday responsibilities of life! Faith that does not result in faithfulness will not accomplish God's work. It is good to have faith to do the *difficult* (Luke 17:1–3) and the *impossible* (Luke 17:4–6), but it is essential that we have faith to do even the *routine tasks* our Master has committed to us. Privileges must always be balanced with responsibilities.

The servant in the story was evidently a "jack-of-all-trades," for he was responsible for farming, shepherding, and cooking. It was not unusual for people with only modest means to hire at least one servant.

—*Be Courageous*, pages 61–62

6. Review Luke 17:7–10. Why was the situation Jesus described of a master ministering to his servant such a radical concept to His audience? What in Jesus' words reveals just how unusual He knew it would be to hear? How is this completely new way of thinking received?

From the Commentary

As His servants, we must beware lest we have the wrong attitude toward our duties. There are two extremes to avoid: merely doing our duty in a slavish way *because we have to*, or doing our duty *because we hope to gain a reward*. Christian industrialist R. G. LeTorneau used to say, "If you give because it pays, *it won't pay*." This principle also applies to service. Both extremes are seen in the attitudes of the elder brother (Luke 15:25–32) who was miserably obedient, always hoping that his father would let him have a party with his friends.

—*Be Courageous*, pages 62–63

7. Read Ephesians 6:6; John 14:15; 1 John 5:3; and Psalm 40:8. How does each of these verses reveal the proper attitude for Christian service? Why is service such an important part of Jesus' message to His disciples?

From the Commentary

Between Luke 17:10 and 11, the events of John 11 occurred as the Lord Jesus made His way to Jerusalem. At the border of Samaria and Judea, Jesus healed ten lepers at one time, and the fact that the miracle involved a Samaritan made it even more significant (see Luke 10:30–37). Jesus used this event to teach a lesson about gratitude to God.

The account begins with *ten unclean men* (Luke 17:11–13), all of whom were lepers (see the comments on Luke 5:12–15). The Jews and Samaritans would not normally live together, but misery loves company and all ten were outcasts. What difference does birth make if you are experiencing a living death?

—*Be Courageous*, page 63

8. Review Luke 17:11–19. Why did the ten unclean men have hope? The name *Master* here is the same one Simon used (Luke 5:5) and means "chief commander." Why is that significant in this story?

More to Consider: Luke's account closes with one unusual man (Luke 17:15–19). The Samaritan fell at Jesus' feet to praise Him and give thanks. It would have been logical for him to have followed the other men and gone to the temple, but he first came to the Lord Jesus with his sacrifice of praise (Ps. 107:22; Heb. 13:15). Why did this act please Jesus more than all the other sacrifices? In what ways did this Samaritan "become" a priest, by what he did (see Ps. 116:12–19)? What did this man gain by coming to Jesus instead of going to the priests? What lesson is there for us today in this story?

From the Commentary

The Jewish people lived in an excited atmosphere of expectancy, particularly at the Passover season when they commemorated their deliverance from Egypt. They longed for another Moses who would deliver them from their bondage. Some had hoped that John the Baptist would be the deliverer, and then the attention focused on Jesus (John 6:15). The fact that He was going to Jerusalem excited them all the more (Luke 19:11). Perhaps He would establish the promised kingdom!

The Pharisees were the custodians of the law (Matt. 23:2–3), so they had the right to ask Jesus when He thought the kingdom of God would appear. It was customary for Jewish teachers to discuss these subjects publicly, and Jesus gave them a satisfactory answer. However, He reserved His detailed lessons for His disciples.

The word translated "observation" (Luke 17:20) is used only here in the New Testament and means in classical Greek "to observe the future by signs." It carries the idea of spying, lying in wait, and even scientific investigation.

—*Be Courageous*, page 65

9. Review Luke 17:20–37. Why did Jesus make the point that God's kingdom would not come with great outward show? How would that have been received by the Pharisees? Why was their question ultimately a tragic one? What's wrong with asking about the coming kingdom?

From the Commentary

Jesus then used two Old Testament events to illustrate the certainty and the suddenness of His coming: the flood (Gen. 6—8) and the destruction of Sodom (Gen. 19). In both examples, the people of the world were caught unprepared as they engaged in their everyday activities of eating and drinking, marrying, buying, and selling. Noah witnessed to his generation in the years preceding the flood (2 Peter 2:5), but his preaching did not convert them. Noah and his wife, his three sons, and their wives—only eight people—were saved from destruction because they entered the ark. Peter saw this as an illustration of the salvation Christians have through faith in Jesus Christ (1 Peter 3:18–22).

Both Noah and Lot lived in days of religious compromise and moral declension, not unlike our present time. During "the days of Noah," population growth was significant (Gen. 6:1), lawlessness was on the increase (Gen. 6:5), and the earth was given over to violence (Gen. 6:11, 13). In Lot's day, the unnatural lusts of Sodom and Gomorrah were so abhorrent to God that He completely destroyed the cities. Only Lot, two of his daughters, and his wife (who later was destroyed) were saved from the terrible judgment.

—*Be Courageous*, page 67

10. In what ways does Luke 17:30–36 describe what will occur when Jesus Christ returns? (See also Rev. 19:11—20:6.) What warning can we take from these verses? How do they apply especially to Israel? (See Matt. 24:29–44.)

Looking Inward

Take a moment to reflect on all that you've explored thus far in this study of Luke 17. Review your notes and answers and think about how each of these things matters in your life today.

Tips for Small Groups: To get the most out of this section, form pairs or trios and have group members take turns answering these questions. Be honest and as open as you can in this discussion, but most of all, be encouraging and supportive of others. Be sensitive to those who are going through particularly difficult times and don't press for people to speak if they're uncomfortable doing so.

11. What are some ways you struggle with forgiveness? Has anyone forgiven you for something you thought was unforgivable? Describe that situation. How did you feel when forgiven? What did you learn about forgiveness in this situation?

12. Have you ever caused someone to stumble in his or her faith? Describe that situation. Why is this such a grievous sin? Has someone caused you to stumble? What led to that fall? How did you recover? What are some practical steps to take so you avoid making someone stumble?

13. What are some ways you serve others today? What is the greatest challenge you face as you consider being a servant? What about serving brings you joy?

Going Forward

14. Think of one or two things that you have learned that you'd like to work on in the coming week. Remember that this is all about quality, not quantity. It's better to work on one specific area of life and do it well than to work on many and do poorly (or to be so overwhelmed that you simply don't try).

Do you want to learn more about God's judgment of the world and become more able to forgive someone? Be specific. Go back through Luke 17 and put a star next to the phrase or verse that is most encouraging to you. Consider memorizing this verse.

Real-Life Application Ideas: When was the last time you thought specifically about Jesus' return? What are some of the things that excite you about Jesus' return? Are there things that concern you? This week, spend time every day thinking about the impact of Jesus' return. How does keeping that in mind affect your daily choices? What might you do differently if you knew Jesus was returning today? How can you balance that possibility with the importance of continuing to live out your daily faith life without worry about the future? Work on those things.

Seeking Help

15. Write a prayer below (or simply pray one in silence), inviting God to work on your mind and heart in those areas you've noted in the Going Forward section. Be honest about your desires and fears.

Notes for Small Groups:

- *Look for ways to put into practice the things you wrote in the Going Forward section. Talk with other group members about your ideas and commit to being accountable to one another.*

- *During the coming week, ask the Holy Spirit to continue to reveal truth to you from what you've read and studied.*

- *Before you start the next lesson, read Luke 18. For more in-depth lesson preparation, read chapter 5, "People to Meet, Lessons to Learn," in* Be Courageous.

A Few Lessons
(LUKE 18)

Before you begin ...
- *Pray for the Holy Spirit to reveal truth and wisdom as you go through this lesson.*
- *Read Luke 18. This lesson references chapter 5 in Be Courageous. It will be helpful for you to have your Bible and a copy of the commentary available as you work through this lesson.*

Getting Started

From the Commentary

Lord Chesterfield, the English statesman, wrote, "Learning ... is only to be acquired by reading men, and studying all the various editions of them."

He was referring to "the knowledge of the world," but what he said applies to *spiritual* knowledge as well. Much can be learned from reading the "book of humanity," whether in daily life, history, biography, or even fiction.

There are several "editions" of mankind introduced in this chapter, and each one has a spiritual lesson to teach us. Being a compassionate physician, Dr. Luke wrote about widows and politicians, Pharisees and publicans, little children and adults, rich men and beggars.

—*Be Courageous*, page 73

1. Why does Luke choose to write about these sorts of people in his gospel? What do each of the characters add to the narrative about Jesus' role in the lives of His followers?

More to Consider: Read Luke 2:37–38; 4:25–26; 7:11–17; 18:1–8; 20:45–47; and 21:1–4. Why does Luke mention widows so often in his gospel? What about their plight made them such a hot topic for his exposition on the life of faith? (See Exod. 22:22–24; Deut. 14:28–29; 16:9–15; Ps. 146:9; Isa. 1:17, 23; Jer. 7:6.) What do Acts 6:1; 1 Timothy 5:3–10; and James 1:27 tell us about the early church's focus on caring for widows? What are practical ways we can apply that lesson to today's church?

2. Choose one verse or phrase from Luke 18 that stands out to you. This could be something you're intrigued by, something that makes you uncomfortable, something that puzzles you, something that resonates with you, or just something you want to examine further. Write that here.

Going Deeper

From the Commentary

As you study the parable in 18:1–8, try to see it in its Eastern setting. The "courtroom" was not a fine building but a tent that was moved from place to place as the judge covered his circuit. The judge, not the law, set the agenda, and he sat regally in the tent, surrounded by his assistants. Anybody could watch the proceedings from the outside, but only those who were approved and accepted could have their cases tried. This usually meant bribing one of the assistants so that he would call the judge's attention to the case.

The widow had three obstacles to overcome. First, being a woman she, therefore, had little standing before the law. In the Palestinian society of our Lord's day, women did not go to court. Since she was a widow, she had no husband to stand with her in court. Finally, she was poor and could not pay a bribe even if she wanted to. No wonder poor widows did not always get the protection the law was supposed to afford them!

—*Be Courageous*, page 74

3. Why was it such an obstacle to be a woman in this scenario? How do these obstacles apply today? What other groups today face obstacles in getting justice?

From the Commentary

If we don't pray, we will faint; it's as simple as that! The word *faint* describes a believer who loses heart and gets so discouraged that he or she wants to quit. I can recall two occasions when I have fainted physically, and it is the most helpless feeling I have ever experienced. I felt myself "going," but I couldn't seem to do a thing about it!

There is a connection between what our Lord said in Luke 18:1 and His statement in Luke 17:37. If society is like a rotting corpse, then the "atmosphere" in which we live is being slowly polluted, and this is bound to affect our spiritual lives. But when we pray, we draw on the "pure air" of heaven, and this keeps us from fainting.

—*Be Courageous*, page 74

4. What does it mean to "always pray" (Luke 18:1) or to "pray continually" (1 Thess. 5:17)? Why is this so important in the life of a believer? How does prayer change our focus?

From Today's World

Prayer is something the Bible speaks about often and in great depth. There are few topics more universally championed by Scripture, in both the Old and the New Testaments. Jesus, in particular, had a lot to say about prayer, which Luke and the other gospel writers recorded in great detail. Today, prayer has found itself a topic for discussion as well as a discipline to practice. Sometimes it's the focus of a controversy (such as in the "prayer in schools" conversation), but usually it's merely accepted as a normal part of the daily life of a believer. We pray because God asks us to and because Jesus modeled prayer. And yet prayer remains one of the most mysterious aspects of our relationship with God.

5. Why does prayer remain such a mysterious thing even though we've had years to study God's Word on the subject? What makes it a controversial subject for some people? What can we learn about the power and purpose of prayer from reading Luke's gospel? What can we learn from our own experience with prayer?

From the Commentary

Jesus did not say that God's people are like the woman in 18:2–5; in fact, He said just the opposite. Because we are *not* like her, we should be encouraged in our praying. He argued from the lesser to the greater: "If a poor widow got what she deserved from a selfish judge, how much more will God's children receive what is right from a loving heavenly Father!"

Consider the contrasts. To begin with, the woman was a stranger, *but we are the children of God*, and God cares for His children (Luke 11:13). The widow had no access to the judge, but God's children have an open access into His presence and may come at any time to get the help they need (Eph. 2:18; 3:12; Heb. 4:14–16; 10:19–22).

The woman had no friend at court to help get her case on the docket. All she could do was walk around outside the tent and make a nuisance of herself as she shouted at the judge. But when Christian believers pray, they have in heaven a Savior who is Advocate (1 John 2:1) and High Priest (Heb. 2:17–18), who constantly represents them before the throne of God.

—*Be Courageous*, page 75

6. How is it significant that the woman in this story came to a court of law, rather than a "throne of grace"? (See Heb. 4:14–16.) What is the point of this story? What happens to our spiritual condition if we fail to pray?

From the Commentary

Unless you see that Jesus is pointing out contrasts, you will get the idea that God must be "argued" or "bribed" into answering prayer! God is *not* like this judge, for God is a loving Father, who is attentive to our every cry, generous in His gifts, concerned about our needs, and ready to answer when we call. The only reason the judge helped the widow was because he was afraid she would "weary" him, which literally means "give me a black eye"—i.e., ruin his reputation. God answers prayer for His glory and for our good, and He is not vexed when we come.

How, then, do we explain *delays* in answers to prayer, especially when Jesus said that God would "avenge [give them justice] speedily" (Luke 18:8)? Remember that God's delays are not the delays of inactivity but of preparation. God is always answering prayer, otherwise Romans 8:28 could not be in the Bible. God works in all things at all times, causing all things to work together to accomplish His purposes. The moment we send Him a request that is in His will (see 1 John 5:14–15), God begins to work. We may not see it now, but one day the answer will come.

—*Be Courageous*, page 76

7. How does the question in Luke 18:8 tie in with what Jesus taught in Luke 17:22–37: "Will he find [that kind of] faith on the earth?" Why would people think God must be bribed to answer prayer? How does Jesus answer this fallacy?

From the Commentary

> Throughout His public ministry, Jesus exposed the self-righteousness and unbelief of the Pharisees (see Luke 11:39–54). He pictured them as debtors too bankrupt to pay what they owed God (Luke 7:40–50), guests fighting for the best seats (Luke 14:7–14), and sons proud of their obedience but unconcerned about the needs of others (Luke 15:25–32). The sad thing is that the Pharisees were completely deluded and thought they were right and Jesus was wrong. This is illustrated in this parable.
>
> —*Be Courageous*, page 77

8. Review Luke 18:9–17. In what ways was the Pharisee deluded about prayer? About himself? How was he deluded about the publican (tax collector)? Where do we see similar delusions in today's church?

More to Consider: Describe the contrasts between the Pharisee and the children who were brought to Jesus. (See Luke 18:15–17.) Why did the disciples want to send them away? Read Matthew 14:15–17 and 15:21–28. Why did the disciples want to get rid of people?

From the Commentary

The rich young ruler (Matt. 19:20) may be the only man in the Gospels who came to the feet of Jesus and went away in worse condition than when he came. And yet he had so much in his favor! He was moral and religious, earnest and sincere, and probably would have qualified for membership in the average church. Yet he refused to follow Jesus Christ and instead went his own way in great sorrow.

—*Be Courageous*, page 78

9. Was there anything wrong with the question the young ruler asked? Why or why not? In what ways was he being dishonest? How does dishonesty affect our relationship with God?

From the Commentary

Matthew tells us that there were *two* blind beggars who met Jesus as He *left* Jericho (Matt. 20:29–30), but Luke introduces us to one blind beggar, Bartimaeus, who called out as Jesus *approached* Jericho. There were two Jerichos, the old ruined city and the new one built by Herod the Great, and they stood about a mile apart. The two men, one of whom was more outspoken, were sitting at the entrance to the new city, so there is no contradiction (note Mark 10:46).

In that day, blindness was a common affliction for which there was no cure, and all a blind person could do was beg. These two men had not been born blind, for their prayer was to "regain" their sight (Luke 18:41 NASB; and note Matt. 20:34 NASB). They persisted in crying out to the Lord, in spite of the obstacles in their way: their inability to see Jesus, the opposition of the crowd, and our Lord's delay in responding to them. They were not going to let Jesus pass them without first pleading for mercy.

The fact that they addressed Him as "Son of David," a messianic title, indicates that these two Jewish beggars knew that Jesus could give sight to the blind (Isa. 35:5; and see Luke 4:18). Jesus responded to their faith and healed them, and what a change took place! They went from darkness to light, from begging to following Jesus, and from crying to praising the Lord. They joined the pilgrim crowd going to Jerusalem and lifted their voices in praising the Lord.

—*Be Courageous*, page 81

10. Compare and contrast the beggar and the rich young ruler. Which is a better example of someone who wants to know the truth? What can we learn from the beggar about how to approach our faith lives?

Looking Inward

Take a moment to reflect on all that you've explored thus far in this study of Luke 18. Review your notes and answers and think about how each of these things matters in your life today.

> *Tips for Small Groups: To get the most out of this section, form pairs or trios and have group members take turns answering these questions. Be honest and as open as you can in this discussion, but most of all, be encouraging and supportive of others. Be sensitive to those who are going through particularly difficult times and don't press for people to speak if they're uncomfortable doing so.*

11. What is your relationship with prayer today? How does it encourage you? What challenges do you face in growing deeper in prayer? What about prayer troubles you? How are prayer and trust related?

12. Describe a season when you were failing to pray. What led to that season? How did the lack of prayer affect your daily faith life? What brought you back to prayer (assuming you've returned)? How does prayer change your outlook?

13. Are you more like Bartimaeus or the rich young ruler? What makes you act like one or the other? What lessons can you apply to your life from these stories?

Going Forward

14. Think of one or two things that you have learned that you'd like to work on in the coming week. Remember that this is all about quality, not quantity. It's better to work on one specific area of life and do it well than to work on many and do poorly (or to be so overwhelmed that you simply don't try).

Do you want to confront the doubts that hinder your prayers? Be specific. Go back through Luke 18 and put a star next to the phrase or verse that is most encouraging to you. Consider memorizing this verse.

Real-Life Application Ideas: Jesus talks about money in this chapter (and elsewhere in the Gospels). But more than actual riches, He's talking about our attitude toward them. This week, take an attitude inventory to examine how you deal with your wealth. Whether you're "rich" or "poor" according to world standards, your attitude matters. As you think about this attitude, spend time in prayer asking God to give you humility and a generous heart in all things related to wealth. Listen for God's wisdom in these areas and put into practice all that He asks of you.

Seeking Help

15. Write a prayer below (or simply pray one in silence), inviting God to work on your mind and heart in those areas you've noted in the Going Forward section. Be honest about your desires and fears.

Notes for Small Groups:

- *Look for ways to put into practice the things you wrote in the Going Forward section. Talk with other group members about your ideas and commit to being accountable to one another.*

- *During the coming week, ask the Holy Spirit to continue to reveal truth to you from what you've read and studied.*

- *Before you start the next lesson, read Luke 19—20. For more in-depth lesson preparation, read chapters 6 and 7, "Jerusalem at Last!" and "Issues and Answers," in* Be Courageous.

Jerusalem
(LUKE 19—20)

Before you begin …

Before you begin …
- *Pray for the Holy Spirit to reveal truth and wisdom as you go through this lesson.*
- *Read Luke 19—20. This lesson references chapters 6 and 7 in* Be Courageous. *It will be helpful for you to have your Bible and a copy of the commentary available as you work through this lesson.*

Getting Started

From the Commentary

The name *Zaccheus* means "righteous one," but this supervisor of tax collectors was not living up to his name. Certainly the Jewish religious community in Jericho would not have considered him righteous, for he not only collected taxes from his own people but also worked for the unclean Gentiles! And publicans were notorious for collecting more taxes than required; the more money they collected, the more income they enjoyed (Luke 3:12–13).

Though Zaccheus was a renegade in the eyes of the Jews, he was a precious lost sinner in the eyes of Jesus.

—*Be Courageous*, pages 85–86

1. What changes did Zaccheus experience that day, all because Jesus visited Jericho? How are each of these changes significant? What lessons does Jesus teach through His invitation and subsequent conversation with Zaccheus? Why would these lessons have been surprising to the people of his time?

More to Consider: Under the Mosaic law, if a thief voluntarily confessed his crime, he had to restore what he took, add one-fifth to it, and bring a trespass offering to the Lord (Lev. 6:1–7). If he stole something he could not restore, he had to repay four- or fivefold (Exod. 22:1), and if he was caught with the goods, he had to repay double (Exod. 22:4). How does this truth add weight to Zaccheus's story? How does it make his actions even more notable?

2. Choose one verse or phrase from Luke 19—20 that stands out to you. This could be something you're intrigued by, something that makes you

uncomfortable, something that puzzles you, something that resonates with you, or just something you want to examine further. Write that here.

Going Deeper

From the Commentary

> Passover season was always an emotionally charged time for the Jews, because it reminded them of their deliverance from the slavery of Egypt. This annual celebration aggravated the misery of their bondage to Rome and made them yearn all the more for a deliverer. Of course, there were subversive groups like the Zealots who used commando tactics against Rome, and politicians like the Herodians who compromised with Rome, but most of the Jews rejected those approaches. They wanted God to fulfill the Old Testament prophecies and send them their promised King.
>
> —*Be Courageous*, page 88

3. Review Luke 19:11–27. How did Jesus answer those who expected Him to establish His kingdom on earth? What kind of king were they hoping for or expecting? How does Jesus' parable address this?

From the Commentary

> In the parable of the pounds, each servant has the same deposit, which probably represents the message of the gospel (1 Thess. 2:4; 1 Tim. 1:11; 6:20). Our gifts and abilities are different, but our job is the same: to share the Word of God so that it multiplies and fills the world (1 Thess. 1:8; 2 Thess. 3:1). Only 120 believers met together on the day of Pentecost (Acts 1:15), but before that day ended, there were 3,000 more (Acts 2:41). And before long, there were 5,000 believers (Acts 4:4). In time, the Jewish leaders accused the disciples of "filling Jerusalem" with the message (Acts 5:28)!
>
> —*Be Courageous*, page 90

4. When it comes to witnessing, all believers start on the same level. How does this affect the reward given for faithful work? What is the reward

for faithful work? How does the way we serve Jesus today determine our ministry and reward when He comes to establish His kingdom on earth? How can we keep from making our service on earth a competition for future rewards?

From the Commentary

God was gracious to Israel and gave the nation nearly forty years of grace before judgment fell (Luke 19:41–44). But we must be careful to see in this a warning to all who reject Jesus Christ—Jew or Gentile—for during this time while He is away in heaven, Jesus Christ is calling men everywhere to repent and submit to Him.

The faithful servants obeyed because they trusted their master and wanted to please him. The unfaithful servant disobeyed because he feared his master. But these citizens rebelled because they hated their king (Luke 19:14). Jesus quoted Psalm 69:4 and told His disciples, "They hated me without a cause" (John 15:25).

—*Be Courageous*, pages 91–92

5. In what ways are we living in the period between Luke 19:14 and 15? What task has Jesus given us to perform in the interim? What will Jesus say to us when He returns?

From the Commentary

> Instead of *praying* for the people, the priests were *preying* on the people! The temple was not a "house of prayer" (Isa. 56:7); it was a "den of thieves" (Jer. 7:11). Campbell Morgan reminds us that a "den of thieves" is a place where thieves *run to hide* after they have committed their wicked deeds. The religious leaders were using the services of the holy temple to cover up their sins (see Isa. 1:1–20). But before we condemn them too harshly, have we ever gone to church and participated in religious worship just to give people the impression that we were godly?
>
> Jesus remained in the temple and used it as a gathering place for those who needed help. He healed many who were sick and afflicted, and He taught the people the Word of God.
>
> —*Be Courageous*, page 95

6. How did the hypocritical religious leaders try to destroy Jesus (Luke 19:47–48)? Why couldn't they touch Him yet? In Luke 20, what was their approach to try to damage His ministry? Why did they keep failing? What does this reveal to us about God's timing?

From the Commentary

Jesus had already told the Twelve to expect conflict and suffering when they arrived in the Holy City. "The Son of man must suffer many things, and be rejected of the elders and chief priests and scribes, and be slain, and be raised the third day" (Luke 9:22). Jesus knew fully what was coming, and He was not afraid.

In chapter 20, you meet the three groups of religious leaders (Luke 20:1) and witness their conflict with Jesus. They challenged Him because He had cleansed the temple and called them "thieves." They tried to catch Him in His words so they could trump up some charge against Him and have Him arrested as an enemy of the state.

But there was more to this series of questions than mere guile. The word translated "rejected" in Luke 9:22 (and also Luke 20:17) means "to reject after investigation." It was required that the Jews carefully examine the Passover lambs from the tenth day to the fourteenth day to make sure they had no blemishes (Ex. 12:1–6). Jesus Christ, the Lamb of God (John 1:29), was watched and tested by His enemies during that final week, and yet in spite of what they saw and learned, they rejected Him.

—*Be Courageous*, page 99

7. In what ways was Jesus also testing or examining His enemies? How did His questions reveal their intentions?

From the Commentary

The cleansing of the temple was a dramatic event that both captured the attention of the people and aroused the anger of the religious establishment. The fact that Jesus daily made the temple His headquarters for ministry only made the members of the Sanhedrin more indignant, so they decided to question Him. "What authority do You have to do these things?" they asked. "And if You do have authority, who gave it to You?"

Authority is important for the success of any social, political, or religious organization; without authority, you have confusion. The chief priests claimed their authority from Moses, for the law set the tribe of Levi apart to serve in the sanctuary. The scribes were students of the law and claimed their authority from the rabbis whose interpretations they studied. The elders of Israel were the leaders of the families and clans, chosen usually for their experience and wisdom. All of these men were sure of their authority and were not afraid to confront Jesus.

They wanted to push our Lord into a dilemma so that no matter how He answered, He would be in trouble. If He said that He had *no* authority, then He was in trouble with the Jews for invading their temple and acting like a prophet. If He said that His authority came from God, then He would be in trouble with the Romans, who were always alert to would-be messiahs, especially during Passover season (see Acts 5:34–39; 21:37–39).

—*Be Courageous*, page 100

8. Review Luke 20:1–19. How does Jesus turn the question around and put His accusers on the defensive? What question does He ask? How does He use Scripture to challenge them?

More to Consider: Review Luke 20:3–8. Why did Jesus take them back to John the Baptist? (See John 1:15–34; 7:14–17.) How did their refusal to submit to John's message influence Jesus' response (or lack thereof) to their question?

From the Commentary

Jesus knew that the men who questioned Him were spies sent by the Pharisees and the Herodians (Mark 12:13), but He patiently listened and replied. These two groups were usually fighting each other, but now they had a common enemy, and this brought them together. They wanted to discuss taxes and Roman authority, hoping to provoke Jesus into offending either the Jews ("Pay the poll tax!") or the Romans ("Don't pay the poll tax!"). But Jesus lifted the discussion to a much higher level and forced the spies to think about the relationship between the kingdom of God and the kingdoms of men.

Governmental authority is instituted by God and must be respected (Prov. 8:15; Dan. 2:21, 37–38; Rom. 13; 1 Peter 2:11–17). Yes, our citizenship is in heaven (Phil. 3:20), and we are strangers and pilgrims on earth, but that does not mean we should ignore our earthly responsibilities. Human government is essential to a safe and orderly society, for man is a sinner and must be kept under control.

—*Be Courageous*, page 103

9. Was Jesus suggesting that we divide our loyalties? Explain. How can we be obedient to God and obedient to man? What are we to do when obedience between man and God is in conflict? How do we determine that?

From the Commentary

> While the Pharisees were still gathered together, Jesus asked them a final question: "What do you think about the Christ? Whose Son is He?" (Matt. 22:41–42 NKJV). This is the *key* question for every generation and each individual, for our salvation and eternal destiny are dependent on what we think about Christ (1 John 2:21–25; 4:1–6; 5:1).
>
> Of course, they knew the expected reply: "The Son of David." They based this on such verses as 2 Samuel 7:13–14; Isaiah 11:1; and Jeremiah 23:5. God had ordained that the Messiah should come from the family of David and be born in David's city, Bethlehem (Mic. 5:2). The fact that the Jewish people identified Jesus with Nazareth, not Bethlehem, indicates that they had not really looked into the facts connected with His birth (John 7:40–53).
>
> —*Be Courageous*, page 106

10. Review Luke 20:41–44. Why does Jesus refer His questioners to Psalm 110? How does referring to a familiar (and likely well-loved) passage change the tenor of the conversation? What does this reveal about Jesus' knowledge of Scripture? Why is this important?

Looking Inward

Take a moment to reflect on all that you've explored thus far in this study of Luke 19—20. Review your notes and answers and think about how each of these things matters in your life today.

> *Tips for Small Groups: To get the most out of this section, form pairs or trios and have group members take turns answering these questions. Be honest and as open as you can in this discussion, but most of all, be encouraging and supportive of others. Be sensitive to those who are going through particularly difficult times and don't press for people to speak if they're uncomfortable doing so.*

11. What are some ways you experience God's kingdom on earth today? What about the future kingdom excites you most? How can you continue to enjoy the kingdom of the "now" while preparing for the kingdom to come?

12. Think of a time when you acted like the Pharisees, testing God or trying to prove Him wrong. What led to that season of rebellion? How did God respond to your challenges? What was the end result of your attempt to be right while proving God wrong?

13. Have you ever felt attacked because of your faith? If you've ever found yourself in an argument over matters of the faith with someone who disagreed with you, how did you handle that situation? What worked? What didn't work? What is your role in defending the truth of Scripture? What is the Holy Spirit's role in that?

Going Forward

14. Think of one or two things that you have learned that you'd like to work on in the coming week. Remember that this is all about quality, not quantity. It's better to work on one specific area of life and do it well than

to work on many and do poorly (or to be so overwhelmed that you simply don't try).

Do you want to become more truly faithful in all things? Be specific. Go back through Luke 19—20 and put a star next to the phrase or verse that is most encouraging to you. Consider memorizing this verse.

Real-Life Application Ideas: This week, consider all the places in your daily life where you face obstacles or challenges in living out your faith. This could be at work, at home, or even at church. As you consider these obstacles, ask God for wisdom in how to respond to them. Perhaps in some cases, you will be led to confront them directly. In others, maybe God will ask you to be generous and patient in the face of persecution. In all things, stay focused on the big picture—God's love for His people—so you avoid putting yourself into situations that cause more harm than good.

Seeking Help

15. Write a prayer below (or simply pray one in silence), inviting God to work on your mind and heart in those areas you've noted in the Going Forward section. Be honest about your desires and fears.

Notes for Small Groups:

- *Look for ways to put into practice the things you wrote in the Going Forward section. Talk with other group members about your ideas and commit to being accountable to one another.*

- *During the coming week, ask the Holy Spirit to continue to reveal truth to you from what you've read and studied.*

- *Before you start the next lesson, read Luke 21. For more in-depth lesson preparation, read chapter 8, "Questions about Tomorrow," in* Be Courageous.

Tomorrow
(LUKE 21)

Before you begin …
- *Pray for the Holy Spirit to reveal truth and wisdom as you go through this lesson.*
- *Read Luke 21. This lesson references chapter 8 in* Be Courageous. *It will be helpful for you to have your Bible and a copy of the commentary available as you work through this lesson.*

Getting Started

From the Commentary

Now it was the disciples' turn to ask the questions!

It all started with the arrival in the temple of a poor widow with an offering for the Lord (Luke 21:1–4). Compared to the gifts of the rich men, her two copper coins seemed insignificant, but Jesus said that she gave more than all the others combined. "The widow's mite" does not represent *the least* we can give, but *the most*, our very all. When

we sing, "Take my silver and my gold / Not a mite will
I withhold," we are telling God that everything we have
belongs to Him.

—*Be Courageous*, page 111

1. When it comes to our giving, what does God see versus what men see?
Why is the condition of our hearts most important to God? How does the
following quote from Winston Churchill relate to this chapter in Luke:
"We make a living by what we get, but we make a life by what we give"?
(See also Luke 6:38 and 2 Cor. 8:1–15.)

*More to Consider: The temple was a beautiful structure, embellished
with many costly decorations that a poor widow could never give, and
the disciples mentioned this to Jesus. What was Jesus' response to them?
(See Luke 21:5–6.) How does this relate to His earlier claim that the
city would be destroyed (Luke 19:41–44)? Why is the destruction of
the temple such an important event? What does it symbolize for the
Christians of Jesus' time? What does it mean for us today?*

2. Choose one verse or phrase from Luke 21 that stands out to you. This could be something you're intrigued by, something that makes you uncomfortable, something that puzzles you, something that resonates with you, or just something you want to examine further. Write that here.

Going Deeper

From the Commentary

Jesus left the temple and went to the Mount of Olives, and there Peter, James, and John asked Him three questions: (1) When would the temple be destroyed? (2) What would be the sign of His coming? (3) What would be the sign of the end of the age? (See Mark 13:3–4; Matt. 24:3.) The disciples thought that these three events would occur at the same time, but Jesus explained things differently. Actually, the temple would be destroyed first, and then there would be a long period of time before He would return and establish His kingdom on earth (see Luke 19:11–27).

Our Lord's reply comprises what we call "The Olivet Discourse," the greatest prophetic sermon He ever preached.

—*Be Courageous*, page 112

3. Read Matthew 24—25 and Mark 13 for two more versions of Jesus' prophetic sermon. How do these passages compare to what Jesus said in Luke 21? How does Luke's audience (Gentiles) affect the way he tells the story? What does this teach us about how we ought to approach each audience with our own messages of God's love?

More to Consider: Jesus' message about the future of the Jewish nation was given to Jews by a Jew. Though there are definite applications to God's people today, the emphasis is on Jerusalem, the Jews, and the temple. What are the clues that this isn't a message about Jesus' coming for the church? (See 1 Cor. 15:51–58; 1 Thess. 4:13–18.)

The sermon focuses on a period in God's program called "the tribulation," when God will pour out His wrath on the nations of the world. Many Bible students believe that the tribulation will begin after the Lord comes in the air and takes His church to heaven (1 Thess. 4:13—5:11). It will climax with the return of Jesus Christ to the earth, at which time He will defeat His foes and establish His kingdom (Rev. 19:1—20:6). How critical are our beliefs about the end times to our daily walk of faith?

From the Commentary

The characteristics Jesus stated can be seen in *every* age of the church, for from the beginning there have been counterfeit messiahs, national and international upheavals, and religious persecution. But these things will *increase and intensify* as the time of Jesus' coming draws near. Thomas Campbell, British poet and educator, said that "coming events cast their shadows before," and he was right.

There will be *religious delusion* (Luke 21:8), and even God's people will be in danger of being deceived. Satan is a counterfeiter who for centuries has led people astray by deceiving their minds and blinding their hearts (2 Cor. 4:1–6; 11:1–4, 13–15). Israel was often seduced into sin by false prophets, and the church has had its share of false teachers (2 Peter 2).

Most people are naturally concerned about the future, especially when world events are threatening; therefore, religious racketeers can prey on them and take advantage of them. In every age, there are those who either claim to be the Christ or claim to know when He will return. These false prophets often "use" the Scriptures to "prove" the accuracy of their predictions, in spite of the fact that Jesus clearly stated that nobody knows the time of His return (Matt. 24:36–44).

—*Be Courageous*, pages 113–14

4. Review Luke 21:8–19. What is Jesus' admonition to those who try to prove the accuracy of their predictions? Why would anyone be deceived by their prophecies?

From Today's World

When the Left Behind novels appeared in the public eye a few years ago, much attention was given to how powerful they were in bringing people to Christ. Their popularity also sparked a conversation about the validity of the theology they presented. There are a number of different theological interpretations of the book of Revelation, only one of which is represented in the novels. Whether or not you subscribe to the beliefs presented there, it's difficult to argue the impact the books had on a large population of believers and nonbelievers alike. Of course, those aren't the only books to explore the end of all things. Many novels (and nonfiction works) provide their own views on current and near-future events and how they offer evidence that Jesus is coming back soon.

5. What is our fascination with the end times? Why are there so many modern-day prophets (usually fiction authors) who believe they know how the world will end? What does this say about our Christian culture today? In what ways are these kinds of prophetic claims helpful for God's plan? How might they actually be unhelpful?

From the Commentary

There will also be *international distress* (Luke 21:9–11). I have a friend who has been keeping track of the earthquakes that have occurred in recent years. Another prophetic student has a list of all the wars and attempted invasions. Both have overlooked the fact that Jesus said that wars, earthquakes, pestilences, and famines *by themselves* are not signs of His soon return. These things have been going on throughout the history of the world.

—*Be Courageous*, page 114

6. Compare the events in Matthew 24:1–14 and Revelation 6. How do these reflect the kind of "distress" and "anguish" Luke is referring to in 21:23–25? What is Jesus' admonition to His people in light of all this distress?

From the Commentary

Notice the encouragements Jesus gives to all who suffer persecution. To begin with, we must remember that when we are persecuted, we suffer *for His name's sake* (Luke 21:12), and this is a high honor (Acts 5:41). It is not important what people say about our names, but it is important that the name of Christ be glorified.

Second, times of suffering provide opportunities for witness (Luke 21:13–15). The apostles made good use of the witness stand when they were arrested and taken before the council (Acts 4—5), and Christ's servants and martyrs down through the centuries have followed their example. The English word *martyr* comes from the Greek word *martus*, which means "a witness" (see 1 Peter 3:13–17).

—*Be Courageous*, page 115

7. How do times of suffering provide opportunities for witness? How has this been true in church history? How can knowing this help us as we prepare for an uncertain future? When we are persecuted, what does God promise for us?

From the Commentary

> While many Christians today enjoy freedom from official persecution, or even family opposition, there are others who suffer greatly for their faith, and what our Lord said here is an encouragement to them. A friend of mine ministered in Eastern Europe, and a believer in Poland said to him, "We are praying for you Christians in the Western world *because you have it too easy.* The Lord must help you not to compromise."
>
> —*Be Courageous*, page 116

8. Are the things Jesus described signs of His imminent arrival? Why or why not? How will these events play out the closer we get to Jesus' coming? What is Jesus' message for us as we near His return?

More to Consider: The paragraph in 21:22–24 is peculiar to Luke; there is no parallel in Matthew or Mark, despite the similar language in Matthew 24:16–21 and Mark 13:14–17.

Luke's account refers not to a distant event but to the destruction of Jerusalem by Titus and the Roman army in AD 70, just forty years from that time (see Luke 19:41–44). The Jewish historian Josephus claimed that the Romans killed nearly a million people and took over one hundred thousand captives when Titus captured the city. In what ways was this event a dress rehearsal for what will happen when Satan vents his anger on Israel? (See Rev. 12:7–17.)

From the Commentary

Revelation 15—19 describes the frightening judgment signs that God will send on the earth during the last half of the "time of Jacob's trouble" (Jer. 30:7). When these things occur, it will be evidence that the Lord's coming is drawing near. The image of "waves roaring" describes nations rising and falling like waves in a storm (Ps. 46:1–6; Rev. 17:15). It will be an awesome time, and the population of the earth will tremble with fear, but men will not repent of their sins and turn to God by faith (Rev. 9:20–21; 16:9–11).

Matthew 24:29 informs us that the sun and moon will be darkened and the stars will fall (Isa. 13:10; 34:4; Joel 2:10,

31; 3:15). Matthew 24:30 states that "the sign of the Son of man" will appear in heaven. We do not know what this "sign" is, but it will produce fear among the nations of the earth. However, then Jesus Christ will appear, and every eye will see Him (Rev. 1:7). The nation of Israel will at last recognize their Messiah, repent, believe, and be saved (Zech. 12:10–14; and see Mark 14:61–62).

—*Be Courageous*, pages 117–18

9. How will the people of the world respond to the signs Jesus speaks about? How does this contrast with the way His followers will respond? Do believers look for signs or a Savior? What's the difference?

From the Commentary

In the Bible, the fig tree is often an image of Israel (Hos. 9:10; Luke 13:6–10). Some students interpret this parable to mean that the emergence of the state of Israel on May 15, 1948, was the "sign" that the Lord would soon return. Surely it is a significant thing that Israel is now a free nation after so many centuries of political bondage. But

Luke added "and all the trees" (Luke 21:29), suggesting that more than one nation is involved. Perhaps Jesus was saying that *the rise of nationalism around the world* is the thing to watch. In recent years we have certainly seen the growth of nationalism and the emergence of new nations, and this may be a "sign" that the coming of the Lord is near.

However, the basic idea here is that of *knowing what is going on*. As the budding of the trees indicates that summer is near, so the occurring of these signs indicates that the Lord's return is near (see Luke 12:54–57 for a similar passage).

—*Be Courageous*, page 119

10. Review Luke 21:29–39. To what "generation" does Luke 21:32 apply? Explain. What is the most important thing in this passage for believers to know? (See also Josh. 23:14.)

Looking Inward

Take a moment to reflect on all that you've explored thus far in this study of Luke 21. Review your notes and answers and think about how each of these things matters in your life today.

Tips for Small Groups: To get the most out of this section, form pairs or trios and have group members take turns answering these questions. Be honest and as open as you can in this discussion, but most of all, be encouraging and supportive of others. Be sensitive to those who are going through particularly difficult times and don't press for people to speak if they're uncomfortable doing so.

11. What aspects of the end times are most interesting to you? What impact do these events have on how you live your life today? What do you most want to understand about the end times?

12. Are you more hopeful or more afraid as you consider the uncertain events that will unfold before Jesus returns? How can you use both that hope and that fear to prepare your heart for whatever comes? How can they help you as you share your faith with nonbelievers?

13. Do you see any signs that we're in the end times? What are those signs? How do you know they're signs? How does identifying signs or believing you're in the end times bring you closer to Christ?

Going Forward

14. Think of one or two things that you have learned that you'd like to work on in the coming week. Remember that this is all about quality, not quantity. It's better to work on one specific area of life and do it well than to work on many and do poorly (or to be so overwhelmed that you simply don't try).

Do you want to be better prepared for Jesus' return? Be specific. Go back through Luke 21 and put a star next to the phrase or verse that is most encouraging to you. Consider memorizing this verse.

Real-Life Application Ideas: This week, invite a few friends to do an informal study of end-times theologies. Ask a pastor or church leader for some resources. Then seek out some of your own online or at a local library. Make it your goal to examine the most notable theologies, and to discuss them in a healthy, affirming way with the other members of your small group. Ask yourself these questions: What's most important to take away from this study? Why is there such disagreement among scholars about what's true? How can we grow closer to Christ through a study of end times, rather than turn this into a debate about who's right?

Seeking Help

15. Write a prayer below (or simply pray one in silence), inviting God to work on your mind and heart in those areas you've noted in the Going Forward section. Be honest about your desires and fears.

Notes for Small Groups:

- *Look for ways to put into practice the things you wrote in the Going Forward section. Talk with other group members about your ideas and commit to being accountable to one another.*

- *During the coming week, ask the Holy Spirit to continue to reveal truth to you from what you've read and studied.*

- *Before you start the next lesson, read Luke 22. For more in-depth lesson preparation, read chapters 9 and 10, "In the Upper Room" and "The Night They Arrested God," in* Be Courageous.

The Arrest
(LUKE 22)

Before you begin ...
- *Pray for the Holy Spirit to reveal truth and wisdom as you go through this lesson.*
- *Read Luke 22. This lesson references chapters 9 and 10 in* Be Courageous. *It will be helpful for you to have your Bible and a copy of the commentary available as you work through this lesson.*

Getting Started

From the Commentary

Jesus had steadfastly "set his face to go to Jerusalem" (Luke 9:51), knowing full well what would happen to Him there, and now those events were about to occur.

They were appointments, not accidents, for they had been determined by the Father and written centuries ago in the Old Testament Scriptures (Luke 24:26–27). We cannot but admire our Savior and love Him more as we see

Him courageously enter into this time of suffering and eventual death. We must remember that He did it for us.

The Passover supper in the upper room gives us the focus for our present study.

Passover, Pentecost, and Tabernacles were the three most important feasts on the Jewish calendar (Lev. 23), and all the Jewish men were expected to go to Jerusalem each year to celebrate (Deut. 16:16). The Feast of Passover commemorated the deliverance of Israel from Egypt, and it was a time for both remembering and rejoicing (Ex. 11—12). Thousands of excited pilgrims crowded in and around Jerusalem during that week, always causing the Romans to be nervous about possible uprisings.

—*Be Courageous*, page 123

1. Review Luke 22:1–13. Why is it significant that Passover had strong political overtones? How would that have been the ideal time for a would-be messiah to attempt to overthrow Rome? How does this explain the presence of Pontius Pilate and King Herod in Jerusalem, instead of in their respective headquarters?

More to Consider: It is incredible that the religious leaders perpetrated history's greatest crime during Israel's holiest festival. During Passover, the Jews were expected to remove all leaven (yeast) from their houses (Exod. 12:15) as a reminder that their ancestors left Egypt in haste and had to eat unleavened bread. How does this shed light on Jesus' warning about the "yeast of the Pharisees" (Luke 12:1; and see Matt. 16:6; 1 Cor. 5:1–8)? How do we see the hypocrisy of the Pharisees at work during this period of history?

2. Choose one verse or phrase from Luke 22 that stands out to you. This could be something you're intrigued by, something that makes you uncomfortable, something that puzzles you, something that resonates with you, or just something you want to examine further. Write that here.

Going Deeper

From the Commentary

> Until the disciples arrived at the upper room, only Jesus and Peter and John had known where the feast would be held. Had Judas known, he might have been tempted to inform the authorities.

Peter and John would have no trouble locating the man with the water pitcher, because men rarely carried pitchers of water. This was the task of the women. Like the men who owned the ass and colt (Luke 19:28–34), this anonymous man was a disciple of Jesus who made his house available to the Master for His last Passover.

Peter and John would purchase an approved lamb and take it to the temple to be slain. Then they would take the lamb and the other elements of the supper to the house where they planned to meet, and there the lamb would be roasted. The table would be furnished with wine, unleavened bread, and the paste of bitter herbs that reminded the Jews of their long and bitter bondage in Egypt (see Ex. 12:1–28).

—*Be Courageous*, page 125

3. Review Luke 22:7–13. How does the way Jesus arranged for the Passover feast indicate that He knew there were plots afoot? Why didn't He confront the plotters directly or attempt to evade them if He knew? What does this reveal about Jesus' trust of His Father?

From the Commentary

The disciples did not know what to expect as they met in the upper room, but it turned out to be an evening of painful revelation. Jesus, the Host of the supper, met them with the traditional kiss of peace (He kissed Judas!), and then the men reclined around the table, Judas at our Lord's left and John at His right (John 13:23).

He taught them by what He *said* and by what He *did*. He told His friends that He had a great desire to share this last Passover with them before He suffered. Passover commemorated the exodus of Israel from Egypt centuries before, but He would accomplish a greater "exodus" on the cross. He would purchase redemption from sin for a world of lost sinners (Luke 9:31).

Then He arose, girded Himself with a towel, and washed the disciples' feet, including Judas's (John 13:1–20). Later that evening, the Twelve would argue over which of them was the greatest, so this lesson on humility and service did not penetrate their hearts. Perhaps Peter had this scene in mind when years later he admonished his readers to "be clothed with humility" (1 Peter 5:5; and see Phil. 2:1–11).

—*Be Courageous*, pages 126–27

4. How do Jesus' words in Luke 22:16 indicate that there would be no more Passover? What would the next feast be? (See Luke 22:28–30; 13:24–30; Matt. 8:11–12.) In what ways was Jesus seeing beyond the suffering to the glory? How can we do that today?

From the Commentary

> Jesus had already hinted to His disciples that one of their
> number was not truly with Him (John 6:66–71), but now
> He openly spoke about a traitor in their midst. However,
> He did not do this just for the sake of the disciples, but
> more for the sake of Judas. Jesus had kissed Judas and
> washed his feet, and now He was giving Judas another
> opportunity to repent. It is most significant that Jesus did
> not openly identify Judas as the traitor but protected him
> until the very end.
>
> —*Be Courageous*, page 127

5. Review Luke 22:21–23. If Jesus knew that Judas would betray Him,
why did He choose him in the first place? And if somebody had to betray
the Lord, why condemn Judas? After all, didn't he simply do God's will
and fulfill the Old Testament prophecy? (See Pss. 41:9; 55:12–14; compare
Pss. 69:25 and 109:8 with Acts 1:15–20.) Did the selection of Judas seal his
fate or give him the opportunity to believe? Explain.

From the Commentary

It is interesting that the word of warning in 22:31–38 followed the dispute over who was the greatest! Imagine how the disciples must have felt when they heard that not only would one of their number betray Him, but that their spokesman and leader would publicly deny Him! If a strong man like Peter was going to fail the Lord, what hope was there for the rest of them?

The word *you* in Luke 22:31 is plural; Satan asked to have all the disciples so he might sift them like wheat. These men had been with Jesus in His trials (Luke 22:28), and He would not forsake them in their trials. This was both a warning and an encouragement to Peter and the other men, and our Lord's prayers were answered. Peter's courage failed but not his faith; he was restored to fellowship with Christ and was greatly used to strengthen God's people.

—*Be Courageous*, page 129

6. What warning does Peter's boasting give us about knowing our own hearts? (See Jer. 17:9.) How did he fail in his greatest point of strength? How do we do that today? What does that say about trusting in our own strength?

From the Commentary

Jesus stated one of the purposes for the Supper: "in remembrance of me" (1 Cor. 11:24–25). It is a memorial feast to remind the believer that Jesus Christ gave His body and blood for the redemption of the world. There is no suggestion in the accounts of the Supper that anything "miraculous" took place when Jesus blessed the bread and the cup. The bread remained bread and the wine remained wine, and the physical act of receiving the elements did not do anything special to the eleven disciples. When we partake, we identify ourselves with His body and blood (1 Cor. 10:16), but there is no suggestion here that we receive His body and blood.

A second purpose for the supper is the proclaiming of His death until He returns (1 Cor. 11:26). The Supper encourages us to *look back* with love and adoration to what He did for us on the cross and to *look forward* with hope and anticipation to His coming again. Since we must be careful not to come to the Lord's Table with known sin in our lives, the Supper should also be an occasion for *looking within*, examining our hearts, and confessing our sins (1 Cor. 11:27–32).

A third blessing from the Supper is the reminder of the unity of the church: We are "one loaf" (1 Cor. 10:17). It is "the *Lord's* Supper" and is not the exclusive property of any Christian denomination. Whenever we share in the Supper, we are identifying with Christians everywhere and are reminded of our obligation to "keep the unity of the Spirit in the bond of peace" (Eph. 4:3).

—*Be Courageous*, page 132

7. What is the lesson in each "blessing" the Supper provides? What does it take for us to receive a spiritual blessing from the Supper today?

From the Commentary

The Son of Man left the upper room and went with His disciples to the garden of Gethsemane on the Mount of Olives. This was His customary place of retirement when in Jerusalem (Luke 21:37). Knowing that the Lord would be there (John 18:1–2), Judas led his band of Roman soldiers and temple guards into the garden to arrest Jesus, who willingly yielded Himself into their hands....

John informs us that when Jesus went to the garden, He crossed the Kidron brook (John 18:1). John may have had in mind King David's experience when he left Jerusalem and fled from his son Absalom (2 Sam. 15; and note especially v. 23). Both David and Jesus were throneless kings, accompanied by their closest friends and rejected by their own people.

—Be Courageous, pages 137–38

8. Read Luke 22:39. The name Kidron from 2 Samuel 15:23 means "murky, dark," and Gethsemane means "olive press." How might these names be significant? Why would there be a parallel between David and Jesus? How does this tie together the past and the present for the early Christians? Why is this important today, particularly as we consider the role of God's Word in our lives?

More to Consider: Read Genesis 2:7–25 and Revelation 21:1—22:7. How might these verses shed light on the reason Jesus went to a garden before he was arrested and crucified? What is unique about what happens in this garden, Gethsemane?

From the Commentary

Someone has defined "kiss" as "the contraction of the mouth due to the enlargement of the heart." But not all kisses are born out of a loving heart, for kisses can also be deceitful. In the case of Judas, his kiss was the basest kind of hypocrisy and treachery.

It was customary in that day for disciples to greet their teachers with a loving and respectful kiss. Judas used the kiss as a sign to tell the arresting officers who Jesus was (Matt. 26:48–49). Jesus had taught in the temple day after day, and yet the temple guards could not recognize Him!

The presence of such a large group of armed soldiers shows how little Judas really knew about the Lord Jesus. Did he think that Jesus would try to run away or perhaps hide somewhere in the garden? Judas must have expected Jesus and the disciples to resist arrest; otherwise he would not have enlisted so much help. Perhaps he feared that Jesus might perform a miracle, but even if He did, what can a group of armed men do against the power of almighty God?

—*Be Courageous*, page 140

9. In what ways was Judas just like Satan, who entered into him (see John 8:44; 13:27)? How did he defile the things that he touched? What message is there for believers today in Judas's story? Did he have a choice in his actions? Why or why not?

From the Commentary

Jesus had not yet officially been declared guilty, and yet the soldiers were permitted to mock Him and abuse Him. Here they mocked His claim to being a prophet; later they would mock His claim to being a king (John 19:1–3). But their mockery, sinful as it was, actually fulfilled Christ's own promise (Matt. 20:19). He is an example to us of how we should behave when sinners ridicule us and our faith (see 1 Peter 2:18–25).

It is generally believed that the Jewish council could not vote on capital offenses at night, so the chief priests, scribes, and elders had to assemble again as soon as it was day. Whether this ruling was in force in our Lord's day, we are not sure, but it does explain the early morning meeting of the Sanhedrin.

This was the climax of the religious trial, and the key issue was, "Is Jesus of Nazareth the Christ of God?" They were sure His claims were false and that He was guilty of blasphemy, and the penalty for blasphemy was death (Lev. 24:10–16).

—*Be Courageous*, page 145

10. Review Luke 22:63–71. What was the key issue of the religious trial? What was the penalty for blasphemy? (See Lev. 24:10–16.) Jesus knew the hearts of His accusers, their unbelief and intellectual dishonesty (Luke 20:1–8). Why, then, would it have been futile to preach a sermon or enter into a debate? (See John 12:37–43; 9:39–41.)

Looking Inward

Take a moment to reflect on all that you've explored thus far in this study of Luke 22. Review your notes and answers and think about how each of these things matters in your life today.

> *Tips for Small Groups: To get the most out of this section, form pairs or trios and have group members take turns answering these questions. Be honest and as open as you can in this discussion, but most of all, be encouraging and supportive of others. Be sensitive to those who are going through particularly difficult times and don't press for people to speak if they're uncomfortable doing so.*

11. Do you find it easy or difficult to see beyond current suffering to a future glory? How do you hold on to future hope in the midst of present challenges? What role does God's Word play in that process?

12. Have you ever betrayed Jesus when talking to a friend or stranger? If so, what prompted your decision to deny His role in your life? Why is it difficult sometimes to stand up for your faith? Where can you turn to find the confidence to speak boldly and sincerely about your relationship with Jesus?

13. Describe a time when you were experiencing doubts about Jesus. What prompted that doubting season? What did you learn from that time? How did God reveal Himself to you when you were struggling to believe?

Going Forward

14. Think of one or two things that you have learned that you'd like to work on in the coming week. Remember that this is all about quality, not quantity. It's better to work on one specific area of life and do it well than to work on many and do poorly (or to be so overwhelmed that you simply don't try).

Do you want to follow Jesus even when you're being tested? Be specific. Go back through Luke 22 and put a star next to the phrase or verse that is most encouraging to you. Consider memorizing this verse.

Real-Life Application Ideas: This week, you get to be Judas. Well, not exactly, of course, but use this time to look closely at how you've lived out your faith life, and see if there are any places where you betrayed Jesus, perhaps in conversation with others, or in your actions. Unlike Judas, we have the opportunity to learn from our sins and turn back toward God. As you consider your darkest moments, share them with a close friend and talk about what you learned about yourself and about God during those times. Then ask God to keep you on the right path as you continue to pursue a life of obedience and faith.

Seeking Help

15. Write a prayer below (or simply pray one in silence), inviting God to work on your mind and heart in those areas you've noted in the Going Forward section. Be honest about your desires and fears.

Notes for Small Groups:

- *Look for ways to put into practice the things you wrote in the Going Forward section. Talk with other group members about your ideas and commit to being accountable to one another.*

- *During the coming week, ask the Holy Spirit to continue to reveal truth to you from what you've read and studied.*

- *Before you start the next lesson, read Luke 23—24. For more in-depth lesson preparation, read chapters 11 and 12, "Condemned and Crucified" and "The Son of Man Triumphs!," in* Be Courageous.

Crucifixion and Triumph
(LUKE 23—24)

Before you begin …
- *Pray for the Holy Spirit to reveal truth and wisdom as you go through this lesson.*
- *Read Luke 23—24. This lesson references chapters 11 and 12 in* Be Courageous. *It will be helpful for you to have your Bible and a copy of the commentary available as you work through this lesson.*

Getting Started

From the Commentary

Pontius Pilate served as governor of Judea from AD 26 to 36, at which time he was recalled to Rome and then passed out of official Roman history. He was hated by the orthodox Jews and never really understood them. Once he aroused their fury by putting up pagan Roman banners in the Jewish temple, and he was not beneath sending armed spies into the temple to silence Jewish protesters (Luke 13:1–3).

In his handling of the trial of Jesus, the governor proved to be indecisive. The gospel of John records seven different moves that Pilate made as he went *out* to meet the people and then went *in* to question Jesus (John 18:29, 33, 38; 19:1, 4, 9, 13).

—*Be Courageous*, pages 149–50

1. Review Luke 23:1–25. Why was Pilate so indecisive about what to do with Jesus? What was he hoping to find by going back and forth between the people and Jesus? If he declared Jesus "not guilty," why did he still have Him crucified?

More to Consider: Roman officials were usually up early and at their duties, but Pilate was probably surprised that morning to learn that he had a capital case on his hands, and on Passover at that. The Jewish leaders knew that their religious laws meant nothing to a Roman official, so they emphasized the political aspects of their indictment against Jesus. There were three charges: He perverted the nation, opposed paying the poll tax to Caesar, and claimed to be a king.

Why did Pilate privately interrogate Jesus about His kingship? What was the result of that query? Luke reports that there were three other witnesses besides Pilate who also said, "Not guilty!": King Herod (Luke 23:15), one of the malefactors (Luke 23:40–43), and a Roman centurion (Luke 23:47). Why is this significant? Why didn't Pilate simply exonerate Jesus and let Him go free?

2. Choose one verse or phrase from Luke 23—24 that stands out to you. This could be something you're intrigued by, something that makes you uncomfortable, something that puzzles you, something that resonates with you, or just something you want to examine further. Write that here.

Going Deeper

From the Commentary

> It was a part of the prisoner's humiliation that he carry his own cross to the place of execution, so when Jesus left Pilate's hall, He was carrying either the cross or the crossbeam (John 19:17). Apparently, He was unable to go on, for the soldiers had to "draft" Simon of Cyrene to carry the cross for Him. (This was a legal Roman procedure. See Matt. 5:41.) When you consider all that Jesus had endured since His arrest in the garden, it is not difficult to imagine Him falling under the load. But there is something more involved: Carrying the cross was a sign of guilt, *and our Lord was not guilty!*
>
> Thousands of Jews came to Jerusalem from other nations to celebrate the feasts (Acts 2:5–11), and Simon was among them. He had traveled over eight hundred miles from Africa to celebrate Passover, and now he was being humiliated on a most holy day! What would he say to his family when he got home?
>
> —*Be Courageous*, pages 152–53

3. Why is it significant that someone other than Jesus carried the cross? What might have been the theological significance of Simon's role? How might the experience have affected Simon, whether he believed in Jesus' role as Messiah or not? What is the symbolic significance of someone carrying Jesus' cross?

From the Commentary

Public executions drew crowds of spectators, and one involving Jesus would especially attract attention. Add to this the fact that Jerusalem was crowded with pilgrims, and it is not difficult to believe that a "great multitude" was following the condemned man to Calvary.

In that crowd was a group of women who openly wept and lamented as they sympathized with Jesus and contemplated the terrible spiritual condition of their nation. It has been pointed out that, as far as the gospel records are concerned, no woman was ever an enemy of Jesus. Nor was Jesus ever the enemy of womankind. His example, His teachings, and most of all, His redemption have done much to dignify and elevate women. The news of His birth was shared with a Jewish maiden, His death was witnessed by grieving women, and the good news of His resurrection was announced first to a woman who had been demon-possessed.

—*Be Courageous*, pages 153–54

4. How did Jesus use the women's sympathy to teach them (and us) an important lesson? What prompted Jesus' grief? What was He looking ahead to when He experienced that grief?

From the Commentary

> Our Lord was crucified about 9:00 a.m. and remained on
> the cross until 3:00 p.m.; and from noon to 3:00 p.m.,
> there was darkness over all the land (Mark 15:25, 33).
> Jesus spoke seven times during those six terrible hours:
>
> 1. "Father, forgive them" (Luke 23:34).
>
> 2. "Today shalt thou be with me in paradise" (Luke
> 23:43).
>
> 3. "Woman, behold thy son" (John 19:25–27). [Three
> hours of darkness; Jesus is silent.]
>
> 4. "Why hast thou forsaken me?" (Matt. 27:46).
>
> 5. "I thirst" (John 19:28).
>
> 6. "It is finished" (John 19:30).
>
> 7. "Father, into thy hands" (Luke 23:46).
>
> —*Be Courageous*, page 155

5. What is the importance of each statement Jesus makes? Why does Luke
record only three of the statements? How does this support his purpose to
show Jesus as the sympathetic Son of Man who cared for the needy?

From the Commentary

It was providential that Jesus was crucified *between* the two thieves, for this gave both of them equal access to the Savior. Both could read Pilate's superscription, "This is Jesus of Nazareth the King of the Jews," and both could watch Him as He graciously gave His life for the sins of the world.

The one thief imitated the mockery of the religious leaders and asked Jesus to rescue him from the cross, but the other thief had different ideas. He may have reasoned, "If this Man is indeed the Christ, and if He has a kingdom, and if He has saved others, then He can meet my greatest need, which is salvation from sin. I am not ready to die!" It took courage for this thief to defy the influence of his friend and the mockery of the crowd, and it took faith for him to trust a dying King! When you consider all that he had to overcome, the faith of this thief is astounding.

—*Be Courageous*, page 156

6. Why did Jesus save the thief who asked for salvation? On what basis was he offered salvation? (See Eph. 2:8–9.) What do we learn about salvation from this specific event?

From the Commentary

We must keep in mind that what our Lord accomplished on the cross was an eternal transaction that involved Him and the Father. He did not die as a martyr who had failed in a lost cause. Nor was He only an example for people to follow. Isaiah 53 makes it clear that Jesus did not die for His own sins, because He had none; He died for our sins. He made His soul an offering for sin (Isa. 53:4–6, 10–12).

The three hours of darkness was a miracle. It was not an eclipse, because that would have been impossible during the Passover season when there is a full moon. It was a God-sent darkness that shrouded the cross as the Son of God was made sin for us (2 Cor. 5:21). It was as though all nature was sympathizing with the Creator as He suffered and died. When Israel was in Egypt, three days of darkness preceded the first Passover (Ex. 10:21ff.). When Jesus was on the cross, three hours of darkness preceded the death of God's Lamb for the sins of the world (John 1:29).

Both Matthew 27:45–46 and Mark 15:33–34 record our Lord's cry at the close of the darkness, a Hebrew quotation from Psalm 22:1, "My God, my God, why hast thou forsaken me?" What this abandonment was and how Jesus felt it are not explained to us, but certainly it involves the fact that He became sin for us.

—*Be Courageous*, page 157

7. Review Luke 23:44–49. Jesus quotes Psalm 22:1 in one of His seven last statements. How might this be significant to those in attendance? How is it theologically important? In what ways is Jesus' last statement, "It is finished" (John 19:30), a declaration of victory rather than a cry of defeat?

From the Commentary

The message of the gospel rests on the death of Jesus Christ *and His resurrection* (1 Cor. 15:1–8). The apostles were sent out as witnesses of His resurrection (Acts 1:22), and the emphasis in the book of Acts is on the resurrection of Jesus Christ.

This explains why Luke climaxed his book with a report of some of the appearances of Jesus after He had been raised from the dead. He first appeared to Mary Magdalene (John 20:11–18), then to the "other women" (Matt. 28:9–10), and then to the two men on the way to Emmaus (Luke 24:13–22). At some time, He also appeared to Peter (Luke 24:34) and to His half brother James (1 Cor. 15:7).

That evening, He appeared to the apostles (Luke 24:36–43), but Thomas was not with them (John 20:19–25). A week later, He appeared to the apostles again, especially for the sake of Thomas (John 20:26–31). He appeared to seven of the apostles when they were fishing at the Sea of Galilee (John 21).

—*Be Courageous*, page 164

8. Why did Jesus appear to the apostles multiple times before His ascension? What did He teach them during that time? What difference did it make to the believers to discover Jesus had indeed risen from the dead? How does that difference affect the way we live out our faith today?

More to Consider: We do not know at what time Jesus rose from the dead on the first day of the week, but it must have been very early. The earthquake and the angel (Matt. 28:2–4) opened the tomb, not to let Jesus out but to let the witnesses in. "Come and see, go and tell!" is the Easter mandate for the church.

Why do you think God chose Mary Magdalene to be the first to see the risen Christ? (See Luke 8:2; Mark 15:47.) Why didn't Jesus have one of the disciples get the "glory" of being the first to know Jesus was alive? What does this reveal to us about God's ways? About God's love for all who love Him?

From the Commentary

Emmaus was a small village eight miles northwest of Jerusalem. The two men walking from Jerusalem to Emmaus were discouraged disciples who had no reason to be discouraged. They had heard the reports of the women that the tomb was empty and that Jesus was alive, but they did not believe them. They had hoped that Jesus would redeem Israel (Luke 24:21), but their hopes had been shattered. We get the impression that these men were discouraged and disappointed because God did not do what they wanted Him to do. They saw the glory of the kingdom, but they failed to understand the suffering.

Jesus graciously walked with them and listened to their "animated heated conversation" (Luke 24:17 WUEST). No doubt they were quoting various Old Testament prophecies and trying to remember what Jesus had taught, but they were unable to put it all together and come up with an explanation that made sense. Was He a failure or a success? Why did He have to die? Was there a future for the nation?

—*Be Courageous*, page 166

9. Read Luke 24:19. How is Jesus' question, "What things?" a moment of humor? Why did Jesus ask them to tell Him what occurred? What does this say about Jesus' patience with us? (See Rom. 8:34.)

From the Commentary

So many exciting things had happened that day and so much was unexplained that ten of the apostles, plus other believers, met together that evening and shared their witness with one another. While Cleopas and his friend were telling their story, *Jesus Himself appeared in the room!* And the doors were shut (John 20:19)!

You would have expected the believers to heave a great sigh of relief and sing a hymn of praise, but instead they became terrified, frightened, and troubled (Luke 24:37–38). They thought a ghost had appeared! It all happened so suddenly that they were totally unprepared, even though several of them had already seen the risen Christ. Mark 16:14 suggests that the condition of their hearts had something to do with the expression of their fears.

—*Be Courageous*, page 169

10. How did Jesus calm the people's fears? What blessing did Jesus give them? How did showing His wounds to them provide encouragement? How did Jesus help them understand the meaning of Old Testament scriptures?

Looking Inward

Take a moment to reflect on all that you've explored thus far in this study of Luke 23—24. Review your notes and answers and think about how each of these things matters in your life today.

Tips for Small Groups: To get the most out of this section, form pairs or trios and have group members take turns answering these questions. Be honest and as open as you can in this discussion, but most of all, be encouraging and supportive of others. Be sensitive to those who are going through particularly difficult times and don't press for people to speak if they're uncomfortable doing so.

11. How would you have felt if the Romans had called upon you to carry Jesus' cross? What are some ways you take up the cross in your faith life today? What is the most challenging aspect of bearing that burden? What are the benefits?

12. Which of Jesus' seven last statements touches you most deeply? Of the people there at the cross, with whom do you most identify? Why? How can picturing yourself at that very event help you see the depth of God's love?

13. What does Jesus' resurrection mean to you? How is His resurrection meaningful in your faith life? Can you call yourself a Christian if you don't believe in Jesus' resurrection? Explain. What does it mean to you to live a "resurrection life"?

Going Forward

14. Think of one or two things that you have learned that you'd like to work on in the coming week. Remember that this is all about quality, not quantity. It's better to work on one specific area of life and do it well than to work on many and do poorly (or to be so overwhelmed that you simply don't try).

Do you want to learn how to live joyfully in light of Jesus' resurrection? Be specific. Go back through Luke 23—24 and put a star next to the phrase or verse that is most encouraging to you. Consider memorizing this verse.

Real-Life Application Ideas: The good news of Jesus' story as recorded in Luke is fulfilled in His resurrection from the dead. Easter is our annual celebration of that glorious event, but whatever time of the year you're in right now, plan an Easter celebration this week. Use this out-of-context event to remind yourself (and your family) of the forever-and-always truth of Jesus' life beyond the grave, and what it means to each and every believer—not just on Easter, but year-round.

Seeking Help

15. Write a prayer below (or simply pray one in silence), inviting God to work on your mind and heart in those areas you've noted in the Going Forward section. Be honest about your desires and fears.

Notes for Small Groups:

- *Look for ways to put into practice the things you wrote in the Going Forward section. Talk with other group members about your ideas and commit to being accountable to one another.*
- *During the coming week, ask the Holy Spirit to continue to reveal truth to you from what you've read and studied.*

Summary and Review

Notes for Small Groups: This session is a summary and review of this book. Because of that, it is shorter than the previous lessons. If you are using this in a small-group setting, consider combining this lesson with a time of fellowship or a shared meal.

> *Before you begin ...*
> - *Pray for the Holy Spirit to reveal truth and wisdom as you go through this lesson.*
> - *Briefly review the notes you made in the previous sessions. You will refer back to previous sections throughout this bonus lesson.*

Looking Back

1. Over the past eight lessons, you've examined Luke 14—24. What expectations did you bring to this study? In what ways were those expectations met?

2. What is the most significant personal discovery you've made from this study?

3. What surprised you most about Luke 14—24? What, if anything, troubled you?

Progress Report

4. Take a few moments to review the Going Forward sections of the previous lessons. How would you rate your progress for each of the things you chose to work on? What adjustments, if any, do you need to make to continue on the path toward spiritual maturity?

5. In what ways have you grown closer to Christ during this study? Take a moment to celebrate those things. Then think of areas where you feel you still need to grow and note those here. Make plans to revisit this study in a few weeks to review your growing faith.

Things to Pray About

6. Luke 14—24 continues Luke's gospel account of Jesus' life. As you reflect on the key events in Jesus' story, ask God to reveal new truths every time you go back to these important words. Don't let the story just be a familiar retelling, but trust that God will show you something new and important each time you read Luke.

7. The messages in Luke 14—24 include trust, overcoming fear, confidence, courage, hope, and salvation. Spend time praying for each of these topics.

8. Whether you've been studying this in a small group or on your own, there are many other Christians working through the very same issues you discovered when examining Luke 14—24. Take time to pray for each of them, that God would reveal truth, that the Holy Spirit would guide you, and that each person might grow in spiritual maturity according to God's will.

A Blessing of Encouragement

Studying the Bible is one of the best ways to learn how to be more like Christ. Thanks for taking this step. In closing, let this blessing precede you and follow you into the next week while you continue to marinate in God's Word:

May God light your path to greater understanding as you review the truths found in Luke 14—24 and consider how they can help you grow closer to Christ.